D0498285

Edward Said

His Thought as a Novel

Dominique Eddé

Translated by Trista Selous and Ros Schwartz

This work is published with support from the French
Ministry of Culture / Centre national du livre

First published in English by Verso Books 2019
First published as *Edward Said: Le roman de sa pensée*
© Editions La Fabrique 2017
Translation © Trista Selous and Ros Schwartz 2019

Quotations from the works of Edward Said reproduced
with permission from the Wylie Agency

All rights reserved

The moral rights of the author have been asserted

1 3 5 7 9 10 8 6 4 2

Verso
UK: 6 Meard Street, London W1F 0EG
US: 20 Jay Street, Suite 1010, Brooklyn, NY 11201
versobooks.com

Verso is the imprint of New Left Books

ISBN-13: 978-1-78873-411-0
ISBN-13: 978-1-78873-412-7 (UK EBK)
ISBN-13: 978-1-78873-413-4 (US EBK)

British Library Cataloguing in Publication Data
A catalogue record for this book is available from the British Library

Library of Congress Cataloging-in-Publication Data
A catalog record for this book is available from the Library of Congress

Typeset in Garamond by Biblichor Ltd, Edinburgh
Printed and bound by CPI Group (UK) Ltd, Croydon CR0 4YY

his thought as a novel

Edward Said

Dominique Eddé

I

Edward Said was both an author and an extraordinary orator, who took as much pleasure as he gave from the act of turning his thought into a living thing – into theatre. Standing before a packed audience, speaking low and fast, his eyes always watchful, sometimes amused, sometimes serious – often both at once – looking over round glasses set on the end of his nose, occasionally straightening his torso with a quick movement of his neck or arms, his hands accompanying his phrases with long, mobile fingers, he could turn the examination of a dry quotation from Auerbach or the latest agreement between the Israelis and Palestinians into a moment of pleasure. As a speaker he was an artist. He made skilful use of irony, gravity, paradox, erudition and repetition. He trusted his intelligence to hold the attention of his audience and his charm to win them over; he used his persuasive power to soothe his own deep, albeit invisible, anxiety. When moved by anger, he could sometimes wrestle it into icy irony, sometimes not. At these times, his sarcasm would break out, revealing the full extent of his hurt. Were it not for the help of music, the war machine against which he battled – the combined political and military power of Israel and America – would probably have exhausted his strength long before he developed leukaemia. He had the great courage to place his knowledge and energy at the service of a cause that could never be won in a single lifetime, at any price. Fighting doggedly in a western world traumatised by guilt at having allowed the genocide of the Jews to happen, while having redeemed itself on the cheap at the cost of denial and blindness in relation to the Palestinians, Said managed to maintain his positions without ever ceding an inch of his territory to the anti-Semitism he abhorred to the same degree.

His thought exposes the hasty reader to misunderstanding, because it moves in two directions at once. In counterpoint. The way you play the piano. The right hand is always at work on a construction that never stays still, where conclusions are rarer than they seem and anyway less crucial than the effort made by the left hand to reveal them. There are several tones of voice in Said's work – one that is masterful and controlled, another that is irritated and passionate. And a great silence. This silence builds like a secret between him and himself, between Edward, the rebellious heir to an imperial history, and Said, the Palestinian Arab determined to be heard. As a result, there are two kinds of silence in his work. One is maintained by the domination weighing down on the oppressed, which he must break at any price; the other is the silence that allows reason to catch its breath, to turn against itself, which he must keep alight like a smouldering fire. The first is an enemy, the second an ally. Rereading his work in the light of these twin demands makes it much easier to understand. At the same time, Said's phrasing is that of a music lover. Like his friend Daniel Barenboim teaching Arab and Israeli musicians in Weimar, he knew that music must have a good reason to break the silence. And so must writing. But, in the domain of words, the 'good reason' is never as clear or as audible as it is in music. Concluding his text on punctuation, Theodor Adorno, an author to whom Said refers throughout his work, approached the same issue in a different way: 'In every punctuation mark thoughtfully avoided, writing pays homage to the sound it suppresses.'[1]

A critic, writes Said in his first book, *Beginnings*, is 'a wanderer, going from place to place for his material, but remaining a man essentially *between* homes'.[2] In these words, we see at once the seed of a self-portrait, the misogynist clumsiness of youth – Said's critic is necessarily masculine – and the debatable use of 'but', since it is hard to see how what comes after it conveys the slightest reservation about what has gone before. If I allow myself to nitpick so early in my essay, it is first to alert the reader to the inevitable presence of both irony and tenderness in what I have to say, and also to highlight from the outset the importance of exile, of coming and going, of distancing and caveats – hence the frequent use of 'but' – in Said's writing. His territory is a matter of dispute. On the one hand, it must be defended, on the other, he must be able to leave it – and importantly, return to it. This movement is crucial, to *Beginnings* and to his work in general. It is present both at the philosophical level and in discussions of politics and literature. Where timeframes are concerned, he makes a radical distinction between 'beginning' and 'origin'. For him, the beginning is active, the origin passive. One is part of human history – as understood by Ibn Khaldun and Giambattista Vico, whom he cites abundantly in his books – the other relates to myth. This separation enables Said to kill two birds with one stone, at once answering a question of method and sidestepping, but not ignoring, the abyss of metaphysics. God is rendered absent and little discussed in his work. Human beings begin with human beings. The origin is an impenetrable fiction, while the beginning initiates a future of more or less understandable motives and potentialities. It is a human decision with all its attendant will, arbitrariness, unconscious elements and calculations. It is for the critical thinker to examine the more or less fragile, more or less discernible reasons behind this initial act, from one author and situation to the next. The world Said deals with, as 'a secular intellectual', is a world on its feet, with its back to the void, like the world of numbers. A world that is open to every possible crisis, combination and theorem, including that of incompleteness, which, in the face of approaching death, he called 'irreconcilability'. 'Words', wrote Said, 'are the beginning sign of a method that replaces another method.'[3] This statement implies a decision that is partly beyond you and partly yours. Just as mathematicians declare the existence of numbers and, starting from there, are able to go forwards, so

Said the critical thinker declares the existence of words as the beginning of a system that can be filled and built up in place of the system that is empty, without denying the latter's existence. This accommodation indicates a great anxiety to be overcome, or at least put on hold. Literature and music enabled him to deal with anxiety in sublimated form, and politics to confront it in a combative form that promoted the principles of equality and justice above or with disregard for the pitfalls of human nature. Here we see Said's great difference from his lifelong 'secret companion' Joseph Conrad, who did not believe in progress. However, Said's rigour prevented him from sacrificing his quest for truth to delusion, or his irony to hope. It could maintain hope alongside a return of negativity, anger and criticism, and did so. It reconciled paradox with movement by adopting the compromise formulated by Gramsci: pessimism of the intelligence, optimism of the will. So, unlike Kafka and Beckett, who look straight into the plunging void, Said kept it at a distance, drawing support from the constructions of history. Like a family, academia offered him both comfort and the challenge of liberation – a context to function in and to be shaken up. Security that came with the right to step outside it. His thinking was carried to the height of erudition and synthesis with *Orientalism*, followed by *Culture and Imperialism*. His was a titanic undertaking to fracture centuries of prejudice, fantasies and clichés purveyed by the West about the East. It was a lonely intellectual adventure, at once the fruit of lengthy research and an object of struggle that would doubtless not have achieved the same historical impact had it not side-stepped certain nuances. An entirely new theoretical approach, strongly argued, often comes at the price of a little overstatement and simplification. This might be regrettable, but it is easy to understand. *Orientalism: Western Conceptions of the Orient* is a masterfully delivered hammer blow that marks a turning point in the western approach to the Orient – in other words, in the abuse of power and domination by one self-proclaimed superior culture over another – reaching far beyond the confines of academia. Just as the word 'negritude' has become inseparable from Aimé Césaire, so the word 'orientalism' now belongs to Said. Having become an obligatory reference in that field, Said then applied his method to contemporary events. Day after day, the abscess of the Palestinian issue fuelled his anger and vigilance, transforming him into a brilliant critic of injustice. He became the most fearsome intellectual opponent of Israeli–American policy rooted in the omnipotence of one people over another. This policy, whose every annexation, confiscation and media lie he highlighted and deconstructed, one by one, did not prevent him from simultaneously emphasising the poverty and corruption of the Palestinian authorities. Nor did it prevent him from locating Zionism within the history of anti-Semitism and genocide – he used the word 'holocaust' – thus distinguishing it from any old manifestation of colonialism. However, it did prevent him – sometimes at least – from exposing his ideas to lights that might have enabled a deeper, more complex examination. At such moments, the energy he expended on unmasking and disarming his enemy weakened the force of his critique, turning it into a weapon of riposte and strike. So, *Covering Islam*, written immediately after the success of *Orientalism*, is a book as courageous as it is incomplete, spread too thin on the one hand, reductive on the other. It avoids difficult questions which Said would later explore more deeply. These notably include the Quranic foundations of political Islam, the real danger from the lure of Islamism in Arab countries and the need to find a path separating the temporal from the spiritual. *The Politics of Dispossession*, a collection of writings covering a quarter century from 1968 to 1993, reflects the tireless work of adaptation, adjustment, continuity and correction that he carried out in support of his causes through thought that was always evolving. On this level and on this subject, he was one of the few – if not the only one – to keep going over the long term with so much rigour, impact and flexibility.

The constant loss of territory, both physical and political, inflicted on the Palestinian people is perhaps not unconnected to the weakening of Said's defences and the emergence in 1991 of his incurable leukaemia, which he kept at bay for twelve years. During those years his work did not change direction, but it did imperceptibly change colour. It aged in the best sense. It paled before the limitations of the project that impelled it. It did not desert its combat zones, but it gave music and the interpretation of the past, including Said's own, a central place that was in part released from any duty to convince. At this time, Said came up against the hard core of thought, which in itself resists the very possibility of solution.

Conscious intent receives a backlash from the unconscious and the will is hindered by the weakening of the body. In his final exercise of lucidity, Said set himself the task of formulating that which defied coherence. The beginning of the end is less clear, less sudden than that of the start. Less separate from the black hole of the origin. Exploration of this final time in which one moves neither forwards nor back gave his work the element of shadow it had lacked. In this sense, it could be said that Edward Said's life and work had, between them and together, come full circle. Their shared element of ambivalence and incompleteness appears, with hindsight, as the signature of his personality, his duality, his *completion*. In both cases, there are two versions, the official and the unofficial, the same need for stability and eccentricity, a stated belief in truth and a private awareness of all that its capital *T* can conceal in the way of approximation and lies. The result, when we read and reread him, is the feeling that he thought, wrote, lived and did what he could, what he was. With a rigour and power that were all the more exceptional because he was fighting on two fronts, internal and external, which – music aside – gave him more trouble than respite.

II

I first met Edward in 1979. Our relationship – unfolding in two periods – is not the subject of this book. Nor will I leave it out. I shall refer to those of our exchanges and my memories that shed some kind of light on his life and work. There are many reasons why my attempts to write a book about him have failed in the last ten years. The most decisive of these reasons relates to the difficulty I felt – and still feel, but less so – in adjusting my voice. I do not want to betray us by offering up things that belong to us alone nor to hamper myself by censoring more than necessary the happiness and pain, extreme in both cases, that I owe to our relationship.

Have I really accepted the idea of his death? The idea, yes. His death, no. I am writing this book to come to terms with his death. To try. For ten years, I talked to him, wrote to him, erased him, erased myself. I invented solutions that didn't work but which had the merit of not disturbing my solitude. I went to an island. Our past followed me and got there first; wherever I went, it ran in circles round me like a dog. I let it be, or ran away. I finally read *Nostromo*, which he had so much wanted me to read. (Though it is one of the few novels by Conrad that does not take place at sea, it tastes of the sea to me from start to finish.) *Why did I wait so long?* I'd have said. *Listen to this.* He'd have exclaimed, *I told you D, I told you*, adding, *Why didn't you read it before?* Together, we were every age and none. He stopped acting like an academic and me like a primary school teacher. We didn't care about being adults; we aged when we were silent, grew younger when we talked. We adopted the carefree childhoods we hadn't had. We shared an obsession with beginning. Beginning again. But differently, of course, because we had radically different relationships to time. His was solid, mine fragile. He respected time and cultivated it, got it on his side. I defied it. I asked it for nothing. I consumed months in a day and sacrificed years for a month. We never stopped beginning, improvising, based on the near-certainty that we would never know how to end. Our break-ups never severed the connection between us. Our time was neither solid nor brittle; it held fast the way God or the moon hold fast for believers. When Edward died, the heart of our story stopped beating. I didn't know who to tell, apart from him. All the noise we would have made if he'd been there went round and round in my silence. The sea, trees and seagulls took our place. The only difference between him and me was that I could see them, hear them and feel them on my skin. I was alive, not quite living. He was dead, not quite lifeless. We were still together. Some time later, I slowly learned to train the dog. When I'd had enough, he would lie down. One by one, the days passed, the hours; space was swallowed up between the sea and sky. The world was starting up again. And I too was walking forwards. Soon, I would live the life of a living person – timidly, but still. The beauty around me forced me not to cut myself off. I drew life from the feeling of having lived. Not really. Not only. In reality, the desire to live came to me from friendship, and from my companion Jean.

It is possible to imagine the works of Pascal or Kant without their voices, but not those of Nietzsche and Lacan, nor that of Edward Said. Orality is central to his work. His writing speaks. Moreover, in his work, the notion of beginning is linked to the act of speech.[1] In his first book – his thesis on Conrad – his voice is trying to find itself, hiding behind that of the authors he cites, but already we can tell that it will be heard. In *Beginnings*, it has the tone of a teacher passing on knowledge behind closed doors. Towards the end of the book, in the chapter on Vico, it becomes more political, and more personal. Its power increases considerably with the publication of *Orientalism*, which begins with the riposte Said's voice delivers to the 'authoritarian voice' of Lord Balfour. The 'authority' associated with the 'author' is key to this book and those that follow. What is the knowledge that 'authorises' domination or the power of one people over another, one vision over another? What other knowledge can be used to dismantle the conclusions of the first? All of Said's work is built around this alternating approach. It is present in both his voice and thought. His tone and volume vary from one subject to the next. Based on a constant distribution and redistribution of points made, to be removed or revised, his method always involves him as a physical person. Every time he discusses a novel, a work of criticism, an opera or a historical event, Said puts himself into the discussion. His ironic, critical use of 'we' and 'them' when he is castigating imperialist policy – adopting 'we Americans', which serves as an argument and indeed lynchpin of his rhetorical effectiveness, and 'we the Palestinians or Arabs', which links his past to his present and gives him both intellectual authority and an emotional refuge – conveys a multiplicity of links and viewpoints that oblige his readers to retrace their steps in order to follow him. For Said, identification with different nationalities, communities and countries is only ever a temporary token of membership intended to torpedo categories of 'us' and 'them' from the inside. Identifying himself with different groups at different times, he establishes a rhetorical approach that subjectivises what he says in order to reach the imagination of his readers and persuade them. We need to grasp the great solitude and distance to which the rigour of his choices drove him in order to understand this recurrent need to adopt the possessive pronoun and to criticise it more effectively. As a method, it is more or less convincing in different circumstances, but it did prove highly effective over the long term. By constantly repeating the two personal pronouns, he revealed the deception and danger inherent in the superior 'us' in relation to the 'them' of an inferior Third World. At a time when Trump is in control in the United States, hindsight reveals the extraordinary importance of his words.

Said's capacity for intellectual abstraction can be misleading when it comes to describing his work. This cerebral aspect is omnipresent, but it is not an end in itself. It is transitory. It is the mechanism necessary to deal with philosophy and the world of ideas, to make links between different works and between knowledge and experience. It is also a moment of intellectual exhilaration – a means for which he has the means – that enables him to move from one discipline to another and, in so doing, to rise to the level of the whole they form together. When his subject resists his power of representation, he diversifies his approaches, divides them, enhances their sophistication and overlays them. He adds to his toolkit, exploits the perspectives of comparative thought, without ever abandoning the data of concrete reality. There always comes a point when, however conceptual his argument may be, he inspects it using the fine-tooth comb of history. This point is not unrelated to his initial separation of beginning from origin. Concrete illustrations and the use of details to discuss ideas are his hallmark. Theory in his writing takes the form of an edifice – we could say a factory – that is always evolving and being transformed. This is why, rather than seeking to establish a school – in the sense intended by Barthes and Bourdieu – he wanted his stance and his freedom to be contagious. 'I've never wanted disciples in my own teaching', he told his friend Barenboim. 'As a teacher, the thing I feel I can do best is to have my students, in a certain sense, criticize me – not exactly attack me, although many have, but to declare their independence.'[2] It is true that to be Saidian does not mean much at the present time, a time in which his voice is especially missed. A man alone, rather than solitary, Said the author was only partially cut off from his audience to the extent that his writings address his readers directly and call on them as witnesses. Many of his books – *The World, the Text and the Critic*; *The Politics of Dispossession*; *Musical Elaborations*; *Reflections on Exile*; *Culture and Imperialism* in part; and later *On Late Style* and *Music at the Limits* – are collections of articles and lectures. There is an insular aspect to the landscape of his writings that reminds me of an island chain in which *Orientalism* is the largest and most central. It is the one best known and developed, the most dense and inhabited. Innovative in its thinking and the most consequential. However, it does not necessarily contain the most subtle places, the most attractive corners of his thought. In my view, these are to be found in pages where his interpretative genius draws most strongly on his interiority and works with the greatest freedom in the service of creativity. I am thinking notably of *The World, the Text and the Critic*, published in 1984, *Musical Elaborations* in 1991, *Out of Place* in 1999, his writings on music and some pieces in the posthumous *On Late Style*.

Withdrawing for hours on end to read and write under the inner eye of a very harsh superego, Said found himself through speech. He optimised his relationship to words, supplementing their silent presence with the satisfaction of pronouncing them. He was a modern man, urbane and open to almost everything, a man who never sacrificed precision to haste, who knew a great deal and made great use of what he knew. For him, every minute counted. Every second. Sleep was not rest, it was time wasted, stolen from consciousness and work. Said's work is more than the sum of his books, his writings. It has a great deal to do with his eloquence, his charisma, the way that he physically organised the encounter between the written and the spoken. Between politics and music. Between solitude and society. He invented a style. A unique movement that makes other people's thought spin around the central pivot of his obsessions. In which a sense of digression constantly alternates with a sense of organisation. Infinitely more widely known than read, it was enough for him to speak, anywhere on earth, to become unforgettable. His audience left his lectures feeling that they had taken great pleasure in learning something of serious importance.

Irony offered him protection; humour was more dangerous. He was active on several fronts, in several worlds and cultures at once, and his choices required that he be always vigilant. He couldn't simultaneously afford to laugh at them. His luxury was to test his reasoning against paradox and contradiction. Edward was a juggler, a charmer. He walked an intellectual and political tightrope. He saved light-heartedness and humour for those moments when he felt loved and safe. At those times, he could be very funny. Having myself felt a pathetic lack of humour every time I've been required to defend my political views in public, I can never express enough what the Israeli–Palestinian conflict cost us in that regard. It burdened us, over the long term, with a stifling, repetitive subject and context made all the more depressing by the fact that we were well equipped – on both the Arab and Israeli sides – to demolish seriousness with humour. One day when Emil Cioran and I were walking in Paris, he said, in his inimitable Carpathian accent, 'Tragedy suits Russians, but us Romanians and Lebanese, it doesn't suit us at all!'[3] I can still hear our triumphant laughter that paused only to erupt again even louder. Our sense of the ridiculous was our ultimate revenge as losers over the winners. We reeled with joy. When Edward criticised himself – usually in secret or in private – he was ferocious. It was to knock himself down. On the one hand, he jeered rather than laughed at himself. On the other, he felt the comedy of situations very keenly. He would shake with laughter like a coughing fit and allow his eyes to light up like a child delighted to be a child. He was brilliant at mocking and defusing my sulks and sorrows. I'd made up a crazy sketch for him, a dialogue between an invented duo, James and Marie-Chantal, which he often asked me to perform. I'd invent new things every time, in their two different accents. It was a caricature of us two, close enough to draw on our stories, distant enough to spare our pride. Unlike Cioran – though both were lovers of the insoluble[4] – Edward was engaged on a positive mission. And, unlike Camus, with his subterranean humour guaranteed by the absurd, Edward was happier laughing at nonsense than at reality. He needed a minimum of solid ground beneath his feet. This didn't stop him having a penchant for craziness and nonsense, but always with a degree of distance from the wounded image he had of himself.

Something more about this image. I am trying to understand why the photos of Said used in the public domain often show him in the least natural light. Grave, almost sinister, somewhere between film star and tragic thinker. Yet he also had something of the mischievous child, endlessly curious, ready to laugh and fool around, that made him as much who he was, if not more so, than the thinker with the penetrating stare we are always shown. No doubt this was partly his doing, by *posing*, freezing his image and emptying it of spontaneity. Why? What was the source of this inhibition that was also misleading? Was it a way of defending himself against unknown eyes by showing them nothing of the inner fault line that threw him off balance? Contrary to appearances, Edward did not hold himself in high regard. The awareness of his power of attraction was constantly threatened by an opposing sense of being wide of the mark, not being good enough. The two together were manifested in his face in sudden alternations of joy and dejection that made him unique. 'Charm', wrote Camus in *The Fall*, 'is a way of obtaining the answer yes without having asked a clear question.'[5] Edward's charm lay in something else as well – the way he had of playing his thought like a musical instrument. In his head he was at the piano. His voice, his palette of moods, his hands – sometimes resting, sometimes lightning-quick – his sudden changes of register, indeed his entire physical presence, exerted a disarming musical power. Even when slumped, he was still alert, in control. His smile lasted all the longer because it was suppressed and barely visible, sustained on his face like a prolonged musical note. It played around his lips or perhaps around his teeth, which he conspicuously clenched, hesitating between ending and reprise. When his smile spilled over and spread, it appeared less on his mouth than in his eyes. It was tension, a kind of secret accord between thought and the right to love.

On the phone a psychoanalyst friend – Lisa Résaré – told me about people who are 'fiercely certain they are right'. A few hours later, I thought of what the opposite of that would be: 'the calm awareness of perhaps being wrong'? It soothes me to write these words. I think of how hard it was for us, Edward and me, to not be right. Trust served to heal us, within and beyond passion. Then we would manage to swap the fierce certainty that we were right for the calm awareness that perhaps we were wrong. And to enjoy it. At those times we were immersed in happiness. I should love to retrieve some of that happiness by writing this book or at the least reach that calm acceptance of perhaps being wrong.

III

What is our best way into Said's work? 'A beginning', he wrote in *Beginnings*, 'gives us the chance to do work that compensates us for the tumbling disorder of brute reality that will not settle down.'[1] The movement these words describe is his. It is the possibility, in a chaotic absence of reference points, to find some, to do things differently. It is a maximum investment in a starting point that must provide a two-way connection between an initial intention and its potential for implementation over time. While refusing to abandon either the journey or simultaneous reflection on the journey. To which we can add the corollaries of this approach in the form of repetition, recall from a different angle, the gathering of the differences observed, invention as a new beginning and the amplification obtained, as in music, when a part sung by a single voice is taken up by the choir. Said's entire intellectual undertaking takes place in this back and forth of a future assembled under the gaze of a past that is also in motion – picking up the previous stitch in the next, which in music corresponds to the fugue, where an antecedent is more or less transformed when reproduced. Conditioned by an awareness of return that occurs through constant recall of the motifs of the beginning, Said's writing is constructed like a fugue. With harmonic breaks brought about by the insertion of the present and its political dimension into the unfolding score. The result is a dense, taut and sometimes stilted style that develops its parallels within a relatively sober, tightly bound structure, one trait of which is an absence. There are almost no metaphors in his prose. Or very few. The same is true of fugues. Said does not resort to substitutions in making his case. Comparison is his subject, rather than an aspect of expression or clever wordplay. The result is that his writing without metaphors is in itself a metaphor for thought that is determined not to be slowed, distracted or absorbed, not to be locked in a discipline, not to cede its voice to that of the strongest. It is rare for his words not to hint at a threat, whether internal or external. His moment of escape is limited, unlike that of Proust, for example, the quintessential master of obsession and of the simultaneous convocation of different times, in whose writing a cascade of digressions and metaphors echo one another. In Said's writing, ideas are compared to ideas, authors to authors in discursive mode. Finding it easier to access the inner workings of problems than of lives, his representation of the other involves situations rather than feelings. We should note, in passing, that Said's work was written entirely by hand. It belongs to the twentieth century, which, from Freud to Auerbach, Sartre, Adorno and Foucault, developed its written ideas in ink on paper. In other words, it belongs to a time that remained linked to a physical space while the words were being written. This fact, with others, locates Said within modernity rather than what is known as postmodernity – a word that I shall use as little as possible, since I feel it is too often used to confound manifest differences. Said's work is in no way linear; my book about him will not be linear either.

'Secular narrative, our concern here, is based on – *begins* in – the common and indisputable fact of natural human birth.'[2] In writing these words in *Beginnings*, did Said recall that he had used them, to the letter, a few years before? His birthday, on 1 November, features in the first sentence of his first book: his thesis on Joseph Conrad.[3] So, his beginning takes the form of a nod to his own existence. The tone of his work is set. Said's thought is, from the very outset, bounded by his life. Marked by individual consciousness and anguish, it constantly asserts itself to be so, maintaining the link between subject and object, text and author, exposing itself to the test of time and geography, retracing its steps, not recoiling in the face of pollution, waste, hybridity, the use of 'I'. Combining in one movement both his main theme and the obstacle to it, his thought is a laboratory of the ever-changing relationship between will and action on the one hand, and their sabotage by reality on the other. Not just the reality of events and things, but the reality of the mind that he at first called 'spiritual' (vocabulary borrowed from Conrad), whose inextricable element is entirely contained in the novel's title that keeps recurring in almost all his writings: *Heart of Darkness*. This 'heart of darkness' could also refer to the hard core that Freud comes up against at the end of his life, when the bedrock of the death drive puts up fierce resistance to the consistency of his theory. Conrad, the 'quintessential Freudian hero', encounters precisely this resistance, struggling against dead or demented seas, armed with an ethics that is all the more rigorous for being without illusions.[4] The power of his story in the heart of sub-Saharan Africa, of the slow, endless journey upriver – which is also a journey into the heart of nature and human beings and, ultimately, their common savagery – lies in the powers of a language that plumbs as deeply as possible, with the fewest possible words, the powerlessness of human beings to avoid being sucked into vanity and illusion, and also the density of the enigma that survives them. In *Conrad and the Fiction of Autobiography*, the twenty-eight-year-old Said takes on a subject far more disorientating than it first appears. He wants to understand how creation forges its path in the mind of a sceptical man who is haunted by truth's powers of inertia, by the sinister choice between selfishness and chaos, by the inadequacy of words and the inability of language to halt the infernal course of what Conrad calls 'the knitting machine', the machine that knits time, space, pain, death, corruption, despair and more, an odious thing that has made itself, 'without thought, without conscience, without foresight, without eyes, without heart'.[5] In Said's first approach to Conrad, the metaphysical angle is far more important than that of politics. 'If I were Congolese', wrote the historian Sophie Bessis to me on the subject of *Heart of Darkness*, 'I might not be able to get to the end of that book because, in it, the denial of the other's humanity is so powerful'. Edward would not become fully aware of this denial until his political awakening in 1967. The affinities between the young Palestinian writing in English at Harvard and the Polish novelist who had chosen to adopt Britain and its language are as disturbing as the differences of origin and sensibilities are great. Said had encountered the writer who would inhabit his work to come, book after book. His intellectual 'first commandment' illustrates what he would work to theorise a few years later in *Beginnings* – a radical starting point 'which has no object but its own constant clarification'.[6] At the time, he was still married to the Estonian intellectual Maire Jaanus, whom he would divorce a year after his thesis was published. Poland is not far from Estonia and nor is Vologda in Russia, where Conrad's parents were exiled by political repression at the cost of his mother's life. Said's imagination and his early encounters with institutions – academic work and married life – were miles away from his place of birth. Those early years, as described in his autobiography, were marked by a far less conscious sense of exile than later when, as he discovered and formulated it, he turned exile into a new homeland, suited to his double identity. Cold and dry as a winter sky, enigmatic as the sea, empty of all trace of sentimentality, Joseph Conrad's world would nevertheless remain foremost in Said's imagination for the rest of his life. Why? Beyond all literary admiration, what sign of recognition, what common element in the relationship to self and the world underpinned this enduring attraction that provided a setting for all the moral, physical, political and metaphysical questions that Said would consider until the end of his life? Seen from a distance, the destinies of these two men seem total opposites, as do their relationships to political ideals. The thirty-year-old Conrad wrote to his friend Graham,

> You with your ideals of sincerity, courage and truth are strangely out of place in this epoch of material preoccupations.

What does it bring? What's the profit? What do we get by it? . . . Into the noblest cause men manage to put something of their baseness; and sometimes, when I think of you here, quietly, You seem to me tragic with your courage, with your beliefs and your hopes. Every cause is tainted . . . you are misguided by your desire of the impossible – and I envy you. Alas! What you want to reform are not institutions – it is human nature.[7]

This letter could have been addressed to Said, word for word. In addition to the fact that, thirty-four years ahead of time, it contains the title of his future autobiographical work *Out of Place*, in itself it sums up the world that separates its author from the one who cites him. When he was writing his thesis, Edward was drawn at once to Conrad, who gives morality the individual sense of responsibility, and Sartre, who gives the will the power to intervene in the course of history. In this first book with its subtle dose of prudence and self-assertion, Said is still in a position to observe and wait. Under the surface of an apparent incompatibility, the connections that linked him to Conrad's world ran particularly deep because they always informed Said's sense of irony in the heat of his later political fights. In other words, his ambivalence. In Said's relationship to Conrad the 'shadow line' imperceptibly separating youth from the age that leaves it behind is translated into a form of oedipal separation that simultaneously provides Said with a strong and lasting identification and the right to assert himself in a different way. More precisely, it allows him to keep this intellectual father figure as an established point of reference as he gradually moves towards and away from him. To unhook agreement from admiration, retaining the benefits of the latter without being taken hostage by the former. Despite appearances, this distancing or, more precisely, this critical authorisation, proved cautious and slow. *Orientalism* refers to Conrad more than once, but in protective terms that shelter him from the harsh charge laid against him by the Nigerian writer Chinua Achebe.

True, near the end of this thesis on Conrad, Said provides a first political clarification that carries the seeds of his later positions.

> The trouble with unrestrained and militant egoism as Conrad saw it was that it becomes an imperialism of ideas, which easily converts itself into the imperialism of nations. In spite of the obvious injustice done to those upon whom one's idea can be imposed, it is important to understand that the reason an individual imposes his idea is that he believes he is serving the truth.[8]

The critique is still shaky. He finds it hard to formulate. This faith in truth, for which Said would never stop fighting while knowing it to be secretly compromised, made him write in the same book, 'say the truth to power' and to align himself with the following words by Virginia Woolf: 'One cannot hope to tell the truth. One can only show how one came to hold whatever opinion one does hold.'[9] Can the love of truth become one with a hatred of lies? I don't think so. Indeed, I think that the hatred of lies hinders access to the truth. Whatever the case, it was only in the early 1990s, in *Culture and Imperialism*, that Said would confront his political vision of Conrad directly, writing: 'Most readings rightly call attention to Conrad's scepticism about the colonial enterprise, but they rarely remark that in telling the story of his African journey Marlow repeats and confirms Kurtz's action: restoring Africa to European hegemony.'[10]

One day in Paris, as we were walking over the Pont Royal towards the Louvre, he suddenly stopped me and asked, 'What do you want to build? What do you want to do with your life?' I was twenty-eight at the time, he was eighteen years older. 'I don't want to build anything,' I replied. 'I want to live.' I remember his face, half horrified, half admiring. My extravagance in spurning the idea of a career seemed excessive to him. Suicidal. Another time, twelve years later, when I was struggling to recover from cancer and he just about to begin chemotherapy, he stopped me in the same way, with the same gesture, the same voice, in a street near the same bridge and said, 'We are very complementary, D. I have the knowledge, you have the self-knowledge.' I said nothing, credited with too much on the one hand, too little on the other. I was rather flattered. To have psychological knowledge without knowledge per se gave me the curious sensation of having travelled widely without visiting any countries. I consoled myself with the thought that, all in all, this was better than not having travelled at all. At that time, I was dealing with the fact that my psychoanalyst René Diatkine had suffered a stroke, and I had embarked on a new analysis with André Green. Diatkine had helped me choose life over illness, while Green impressed me greatly with his intelligence. He told me, 'Diatkine helped you give yourself permission in the emotional sphere, we're going to work on giving you permission at the intellectual level.' Since adolescence, I had been filled with excessive, passionate admiration for the intelligence of men, starting – of course – with my father. He was the one I asked, in Beirut at the age of sixteen, to bring me back from Paris Wittgenstein's *Tractatus Logico-Philosophicus*, which I devoured without understanding a word. At that age, I also wanted to marry Sartre. And, as I planned to read every book there was, I had started the Swiss Civil Code, to get it out of the way, so that I could return to literature as quickly as possible. I was crazy. There's a logic to the fact that now, fifteen years after Edward's death, I am trying to use what he called my 'self-knowledge' in the service of his 'knowledge' – immense erudition combined with immense intelligence. Although, to my mind, with the passing of the years, his intellectual brilliance has lost some of its lustre, in return for the pleasure of retrospectively discovering many nuances and fragilities that were masked, back then, by his overwhelming power of seduction and bravura. In return, too, for the pleasure of no longer being terrified by the idea that I might be wrong. There's a new kind of love to explore, when writing and thinking align with love but do not seek to place it on a pedestal. Now, when the beloved other is absent, he can live the life we did not allow him in the days when our love was too strong. Today, my image of Edward has become less of a hostage to the image of me that he reflected; I watch his image free itself as impassively as I watch a blackbird come to the window and then fly away. Narcissism has weakened in favour of what I hope is benevolent lucidity. This too is mourning. However sad we are, there is necessarily something to be gained when there's nothing left to lose. To be gained or given, which comes to the same thing.

There is also something new to discover. When I opened the box that contained his letters, around ten years ago, I fairly soon lost heart, writing in my notebook, 'I had the feeling that the present had entered our past without taking off its shoes.' Rereading those countless pages, written in the days when neither of us could live without the other, shows me something I was unwilling to fully see at the time, and which he tried to make me understand, over the phone, around two weeks before he died. He had just read the proofs of my novel *Kite*, which was published at the time of his death. 'I was very moved', came his voice down the line. 'But you're not cruel enough to me D. You've protected me. Your novel suffers from that. And you don't understand, you haven't written how much I loved you. Mali loves Farid more than he loves her. Farid isn't me.' It is true that I have tended to think my own capacity to love was greater than his. Ultimately, I wonder whether he perhaps loved me more spontaneously than I loved him. Edward was better at thinking than loving. He was an even finer sight when he loved, when his fear of being mocked or snubbed was suddenly swept away by joy, leaving him half delighted, half surprised, like a child who has just got something to work. When Edward was trusting, he trusted more than those who are used to trusting, bestowing in one go all the trust he had held back. And, when he lacked trust, he lacked it more than those who are used to lacking it. In love, he moved as fast as in his thinking – he didn't wait, he let fear and convention go. Near the end of his life he asked me, 'Why don't we have the right to love two women at once?' I reacted with hurt silence. That was stupid. I know, from experience, that you can love two people at once. No particular love – even love for a tree – is like another.

IV

Whether by chance or by fate, Conrad was the subject of Edward's first book and also of the last book written by Green – with whom I used to talk literature when my analysis was over.[1] Green and Said, two men of different political sensibilities – one an Egyptian Jew who had taken French nationality, the other a Palestinian who had become an American citizen – had both lived in Cairo until their teens and had early experience of exile. They also shared a vision of a world without God, professional work grounded in personal ethics, an interest in literature and a deep appreciation of Henry James and Joseph Conrad, two expatriate novelists who had written widely about doubles and the self's relationship to itself. The date of 1 November, mentioned before, was also that of a letter full of praise for *The Mirror of the Sea*, which James wrote to Conrad in 1906. Here is an extract: 'No one has *known* – for intellectual use – the things you know, and you have, as the artist of the whole matter, an authority that no one has approached.'[2] Authority... This recurrent word was crucial to the mind of Said, who immediately observes that these two expatriates, James from the United States, Conrad from Poland, had each had a life of trials and afflictions. 'An afflicted existence', as James put it. Green meanwhile notes that, like Proust, both were novelists of conscience. 'Their aim was to be as present to themselves as possible.'[3] I would say that Said's thought is rooted in the same quest, 'The investigation by the subject of something that has already happened within him without his knowledge.'[4] In Said's case this 'something' is intellectual, relating to life negotiated through thought. He puts it differently: 'The beginning as primordial asceticism has an obsessive persistence in the mind, which seems very often engaged in a retrospective examination of itself.'[5] So that for him, reason becomes the place of both transference of the novel he does not write and interpretation of the novel written by another, which absorbs him in the full sense of the word, speaking to him and making him act, by directly addressing his individual self. Of course, such an appeal can be at once positive and negative. He readily described this encounter that set his thought in motion as 'a magical point that links critic and work criticized'.[6] To say that the word 'magical' was uncommon in his writings would be an understatement. So, what was the magical point that bound Said to Conrad? Said wrote of 'the achievement of an intimate partnership between critic and writer, in which each in a sense is part of the other'.[7] Green observed,

When you take worlds as radically different as those of Henry James and Conrad, you are led to ask yourself questions about what cannot be called either complicity or connivance, because they swim in totally different waters, but they address a kind of salvation along the way that it would be entirely wrong to see as simply grounded in a recognition of value and style.[8]

Born in 1857 in the Ukrainian town of Berdychiv – by then under Russian domination but part of the Kingdom of Poland until 1793 – Conrad was the only son of Polish aristocrats Apollo Korzeniowski and Ewa Bobrowska. His father was a writer, translator and political activist, one of the patriotic Reds, whose activities became illegal when martial law was imposed. Apollo was imprisoned on 21 October 1861, and exiled six months later to a province in northern Russia. His wife asked to go with him. Joseph, then aged four, caught pneumonia, and his mother tuberculosis, from which she died in 1865, at the age of thirty-two.

Three years later, Conrad's father fell ill. 'Not only was Apollo himself dying, but he had become absorbed in a cult of his dead wife.'[9] Orphaned at the age of twelve, the suicidal element in idealism had cost Marlow's future creator dear. There are no fewer than fifteen suicides in his novels. What were the consequences for his life and work of his father's political activism? According to Professor Sylvère Monod, Conrad's guilt was due in part to the fact that he did not remain faithful to his father's ideals. Said took a similar line, while stressing the dimension of shame. 'Although a great deal has been written on Conrad's highly developed sense of personal guilt, not enough has been said of his extraordinarily powerful sense of shame . . . His own personal history was a disgraceful paradigm of shameful things, from the desertion of the ideals of his Polish heritage to the seemingly capricious abandonment of his sea life.'[10] In Green's view, conversely – but not incompatibly – it was the opposite that troubled and outraged Conrad: he was furious with his father's political idealism, which caused the death of his mother. Hence Conrad's implacably harsh assessment of revolutionary ideals:

> Those who think that the overthrow of a bad government implies the inauguration of a better will do well to ponder over these remarks, and the more they reflect upon them and study the history of the events to which they refer, the less will be their sympathy with the revolutionary principles which are spreading so rapidly in Europe.[11]

One thing is certain: Conrad had no time for the world of the passions. Including in writing itself. His own style admits not the slightest vagueness, excess or slackness. It has the elegance, precision and sobriety of a ship steered skilfully into port, without detours or daydreams. Flaubert's style influenced him far more than that of Balzac, or even Dickens. His highly economical use of language had a more decisive impact on *Out of Place* than on Said's other works. This autobiography of Said's youthful years has a

Conradian ironic rigour – elegant, descriptive and free of all orna-
mentation. With the difference that Conrad created a world based
on his own, whereas Said reconstructed his own world in order to
remember and take stock. Keeping his feet on the ground, not
using images as substitutes – very few metaphors. And with an
acute awareness of the colour and excesses that were missing from
his sober everyday surroundings. So that, for the child Edward,
the absence of madness in the Said family becomes the solitary
experience of a world that he must bring into being in his head, in
the anticipation of its discovery. That world is, in a word, the
Orient. What Conrad offered Said was a means of escape. And, at
the same time, a return to the past. In other words, the possibility
of sailing away without losing sight of himself. He offered him an
imaginary arena with moral, even prosaic requirements that
reflected his inner anguish. A time in which two relations to time,
two selves, coexist, one giving life to the other, one looking at the
other. One is punitive, the other rewarding. One is powerless, the
other active. Like Conrad, Said was tormented by guilt and shame.
'Because the present continues in its depressing inaction and
because the past has nothing to show but an embarrassing "secret
action", each tale actually intensifies its own atmosphere of horrified shame.'[12] Reading these words it is impossible not to think of
the oppressive, austere, guilt-inducing atmosphere of Edward's
childhood and adolescence, as he described it at the end of his life.
The time when others slept, and his own sleep was postponed,
became his moment of freedom, 'relieved of pressure and the
continual anxiety of not getting anything right'.[13] The puritanical
Protestantism of his education, the crushing notion of duty, the
small place given to pleasure beyond the somewhat limited role
granted to music and books, the almost pathological deprecation
of sexuality, the constant, not necessarily justified feeling of having
done something wrong. *Out of Place*'s initial title, *Not Quite Right*,
perfectly rendered this dissatisfaction with himself, the repeated
observation that he had done or said something wrong, misunderstood the situation. Said's entire oeuvre is the construction of a

disciplined, resolute, authoritarian ego haunted by a fear of failure. So, the 'magical point' of his meeting with Conrad partly
relates to their common sense of shame and guilt, their desire to
negotiate a way out based on moral rigour, and also the *homo
duplex* Said sees in the author of *The Secret Agent*. A man who
could simultaneously draw on his life at sea and his life as a writer,
reality and fiction, thought and action. When applied to Edward
the same duality can be seen at almost every level: literature and
the world of ideas, music and politics, his academic career and his
personal rebellion. And his choice to be an interpreter rather than
an author or composer is linked to his choice to go beyond criticism itself, to allow creative thinking to emerge and bear the name
of orientalism, like a novel. During the 1980s, he told me more
than once that the novel was gasping its last, that it was a dying
genre. Later he told me, 'I dream of writing a novel about betrayal.'
It is doubtless no coincidence that he was unable to start it until
the last moment, when he could see the ship of Palestine sailing
into the distance, if not sinking, and he was embarking on his
final journey, in a solitary boat, like the one in Arnold Böcklin's
Isle of the Dead. As I write these words, I remember that the first
ship on which Conrad embarked for Asia, as a lieutenant, on 21
September 1881, was a three-master called . . . *Palestine*. The ship
was bound for Bangkok to pick up a cargo of coal, and suffered
misfortunes of every kind for two years, until the sailors finally
abandoned her. This story is transposed by Conrad in *Youth*. In
the narrative, the *Palestine* becomes the *Judea*.

So Edward's end coincided with the writing of the beginning
of a novel.[14] 'The novel is threatened with extinction' – was it his
own death that he was unconsciously referring to? Was the novel
really him? His dead men walking were called Beethoven, Adorno,
Thomas Mann, Jean Genet, Glenn Gould, Cavafy, Strauss and
Lampedusa.[15] All men, as in the novels of Conrad. All single men,
isolated in the sense that they themselves became islands, all
brought to a stop at the point where time empties out. Said wrote,
'Late style is what happens if art does not abdicate its rights in

favor of reality.'[16] His own late style – and we shall come back to this – is a kind of 'betrayal' of the excess of idealism that fuelled his political struggle. And this reversal – paradoxical as it may seem – was a kind of fidelity to his unswerving irony. One of my notebooks records a little phrase of his: 'I have a very keen sense of betrayed ideals.' Did he write these words, or say them to me? Are they his or Conrad's? I've forgotten. It was not so much ideals that Edward betrayed, as the will that often combines with them to make them endure. Having also believed that an ideal could be fought for like a passion, I now write this book with the strong sense that we do not get close to ourselves, to others or to truth without saying goodbye to ideals. Surrendering ideals never means surrendering the rights of art 'in favour of reality'. Nor abandoning the idea of a utopia – possibly quite the opposite, since ideals imply the omnipotence of individual will and reason, whereas utopia requires individuals to dream and to imagine the world differently, without seeing themselves as the omnipotent repository of the means to attain it. Up until his last moments, Edward undoubtedly subscribed to the words of Oscar Wilde, one of his lifelong companions: 'A map of the world that does not include Utopia is not worth even glancing at'.[17] We might add that the land of utopia is to geography what music is to reality and love to death.

There is almost certainly no political fight that does not involve a minimal dose of paranoia. In the best and worst of cases, it takes a developed sense of the enemy and, by extension, a certain sense of persecution, to mobilise your forces, hold firm and choose to battle on rather than give in. Edward was familiar with this feeling and so was I. This made its opposite, the feeling of being understood, all the more important in our conversations. For Edward, let me repeat, defending the rights of the Palestinians never meant supporting the machinations and mistakes of their official representatives. Just as taking issue with the imperialist vision of western culture did not mean that he rejected the joys and tools offered him by that same culture. His knowledge and prodigious capacity for work provided outlets for his sense of persecution and his competitiveness. They armed him for battle, underpinning his capacity to understand and retaliate. He was also totally free of self-indulgence when it came to effort. He did not hesitate to complain, to mercilessly demolish a rival – or himself – or conversely to demand more honour and attention than he received, but he always kept an eye on the time; he never let his moments of regression overrun. When Edward was angry, he was still delighted to be alive. With all that being alive entails. From choosing a tie, jacket, printed fabric or a pair of hand-made shoes to opting for one dish rather than another in a restaurant, or the moment of grace in a concert over that of playing the piano himself, the extreme diversity of his pleasures reflected the diversity of his thought. Not only did one motif not exclude another, for him their value was enhanced through accumulation, juxtaposition and arrangement. In life as in writing, his work consisted in bringing together things that were not an obvious match: Kipling and George Bush, Glenn Gould and Palestine, the ducks on a multicoloured tie and the spotted handkerchief sported in a tweed jacket pocket. With the more or less conscious desire to create a new harmony, every time. In a sense, when it came to reading reality, Said had integrated the notion of obstacle or contradiction far more successfully than that of failure. I see here one reason why he was abruptly brought up short by the notion of 'irreconcilability', which became the leitmotiv of his final years. You have to have believed in reconciliation to be so stunned by the discovery of something that makes it impossible. Let us clarify: Edward did and did not believe. He engineered an inner split that is hard to detect, since his writings call so clearly for hybridity and free movement from one discipline to another. Where does the dividing line fall? It separates his scepticism from his activism, his rejection of capitalism from his pleasure in comfort, and his passionate reading of *Heart of Darkness* from his militant reading of Gramsci. To avoid depriving himself of either side, he maintained a watertight intellectual seal between them. Politically, he fought to win, while inside feeling what Conrad had Marlow say: 'Droll thing life is — that mysterious arrangement of merciless logic for a futile purpose.'[18]

V

Said was left-wing in the sense that he criticised the givens of social, racial and class inequalities. And in the sense that he asserted the power of the will to combat injustice and fate, to design equal opportunities and means for all and to bring about the non-capitalist management of wealth. Nevertheless, his writings remain vague as to the concrete responses and arrangements to be set in place. Unlike his friend Chomsky, Said devoted little space to socio-economic ideas and the fight against liberalism. When he mentions the class struggle, it is in the intellectual tradition of writers like Gramsci and Lukács rather than in relation to reality itself. His fight was clearly focused on the domination of one world and culture by another, rather than on class. He certainly had more than one Marxist friend, but avoided all 'isms' himself. It is moreover debatable whether, in aligning himself with the feminist struggle in the latter third of his work, he truly took its side. Evidence can be seen in his lack of reaction to the misogyny of authors whose imperialist vision he pinpoints down to the last quotation. I'm thinking in particular of Conrad, not to mention Nietzsche. Said was critical of the 'orientalist' writings of Engels and Marx. He cited Engels' words of September 1857, describing the Moors of Algeria as '"a timid race" because they were repressed, "but preserving nevertheless their cruelty and vindictiveness while in moral character they stand very low"'.[1] And he recalls that, in Marx's view, peoples of inferior cultures 'cannot represent themselves, and therefore must be represented by others'.[2] In *Orientalism*, he rightly nails the author of *Capital* with the following citation:

> Now, sickening as it must be to human feeling to witness those myriads of industrious patriarchal and inoffensive social organizations disorganized and dissolved into their units, thrown into a sea of woes, and their individual members losing at the same time their ancient form of civilization and their hereditary means of subsistence, we must not forget that these idyllic village communities, inoffensive though they may appear, had always been the solid foundation of Oriental despotism, that they restrained the human mind within the smallest possible compass, making it the unresisting tool of super-stition, enslaving it beneath the traditional rules, depriving it of all grandeur and historical energies . . . England, it is true, in causing a social revolution in Hindustan was actuated only by the vilest interests, and was stupid in her manner of enforc-ing them. But that is not the question. The question is, can mankind fulfil its destiny without a fundamental revolution in the social state of Asia?[3]

Said notably concludes from this that 'the idea of regenerating a fundamentally lifeless Asia is a piece of pure Romantic Orientalism'.[4] The outrageous image of a 'lifeless Asia' is based on words of Marx's, which Said quotes: 'England has to fulfil a double mission in India: one destructive, the other regenerating – the annihilation of the Asiatic society and the laying of the material foundations of Western society in Asia.'[5] This position is certainly orientalist, but we also know that Marx's revolutionary criteria did not spare western society – far from it. Criticising the self-confident, dominant paternalism of one class or culture does not prevent us seeing those aspects of a culture which, at a particular point in its history, can irrigate it or conversely dry it up. Edward, who did little work on the family and tribal structures in the Orient, was perhaps minimising their contribution to what we

can, in fact, call, 'oriental despotism'.[6] It is not insulting a people
to point out internal elements that lead to regression. Plenty of
work has been done on the constituent elements of German
culture that rendered it porous to the worst ideology possible in
1933. Edward himself, a great lover of Wagner's music, identified
the indisputable reflections of anti-Semitism in the composer's
work with extraordinary precision. There is no reason why an
examination of what led the Arabs to experience a period of stagnation in the twentieth century, with a collective loss of creativity
and a terrible permeability to Islamist illusions, should sidestep
cultural elements that contributed to this decline, focusing only
on the indisputable guilt of the dominant powers. I can hear
Edward protesting, 'How can you link me to a simplistic approach
that I have always fought against?' He would have been right, of
course. All the same, I want to say that, in seeking to be right, we
all, or almost all, have an unfortunate impulse to go one better, to
get the better of someone or something. Because emotions are
never absent from what we wrongly believe to be an emotion-free
argument. I acknowledge this in myself in writing these lines,
knowing that a dose of subjective rebellion is undoubtedly slip-
ping into my reading of Edward at precisely this point. A perhaps
regrettable way of competing, of temporarily 'bettering' his superiority, when he is no longer here to respond. It is true that we
shared an ambivalence that sent us off in a new direction every
time we nearly got somewhere. Not only did we share this ambivalence, we headed into it, the way sailors sail into the wind.
Upholding a political point of view is also an unconscious way of
defending one's own skin. This in no way affects the separate issue
of credibility and consistency. But it undoubtedly sheds light on
motivations. On the relationship to authority. My great political
kinship with Edward is also linked to the way that I am pushing
him here, pushing us both back into our positions. Watching
what we do. If he achieved a balance by devoting himself to literature and politics, it is surely because in these two fields the
individual and society live different lives. In the novel, everything

is on the side of the individual, which is clearly not the case in political thought. Identifying with Raskolnikov does not make the reader his accomplice in the eyes of the law. Whereas, in the eyes of society, the real-life Raskolnikov, unmediated by Dostoyevsky, is primarily a murderer rather than one possible aspect of ourselves. In his writing, Jean Genet went as far as possible to overturn this logic, by glorifying the figure of the murderer, the quintessential solitary man, scorning the collective judgment. Scorning the law. He went where none could follow (certainly not Edward), and in so doing rendered himself totally incompatible with morality. At the political level, Genet and Said had something in common, in the form of their combat against the dominant power of one culture, one race over the other. From this point of view, Israel embodied the same enemy for both of them. But not always for the same reasons. Be that as it may, the similarities end there. Edward was far too rational and 'decent' for the wilfully 'indecent' poet Genet. Nevertheless, the splitting of the self in the relationship to the other – collective responsibility at the political level, the right to be different in the novel – perfectly reflects Edward's dual nature. We were both inwardly convinced that a great novelist's requirement to be truthful was far superior to that of a politician, or even a political thinker. Why? Because entering into a life with the sole purpose of seeing it and bringing it alive affords a freedom that is on a different scale from any project on behalf of the collective, no matter how revolutionary. Whatever good or bad uses may be made of novels and political projects, it remains the case that the former deals with individual solitude and the latter with the mass. Edward needed both. He seized a necessarily limited political freedom and exploited it to the maximum. But what about the novelist's freedom? I would say that he experienced it vicariously, through his favourite authors and, more secretly, in his private life. He did not much like my arguments seeking to replace the notions of left and right with that of humanism. When I said, 'A man of the left who isn't prepared to love, to give, what's that about? Do you prefer him to someone who calls himself right wing and is generosity itself?' He would change the subject, tell me things didn't work that way. In reality he was concerned more with the fight against racist domination than with social issues. The former better reflected the story he had to tell. The same was true of me.

VI

Bound to our Arab surnames, Said and Eddé, our given names in themselves meant we were predestined to meet. He was an anti-imperialist with the name of an English king, and I an anticlericalist linked to a saint associated with the Inquisition. We had to choose: adopt the signification, or fight it. Both of us instinctively chose to fight. We made our names say the opposite of what they signified. Sometimes with so much zeal that it took us back to square one: more than once – and with disturbing ease – he found himself heading an empire, while I became a crusading pain in the neck. In *Out of Place* he writes, 'It took me about fifty years to become accustomed to, or, more exactly, to feel less uncomfortable with "Edward", a stupidly English name yoked forcibly to the unmistakably Arabic family name Said.'[1] I'm not sure I can say as much. I have never become accustomed to my given name, which, even now, sounds like the school bell announcing playtime is over. 'Dominique?' It would have been so good to reply simply, 'No, not Dominique', the way we say, 'No, not today.' In adolescence my given name became a burden. I had to hear it in Doumnique, Damonique or Domanique. In Arabic the only pronounceable, preservable part of my name is 'nique'. And that's quite something in a country where the classic insult – *nique ekhtak* – means 'I fuck your sister'. We rarely called each other by our given names. He called me D, I gave him affectionate, usually Arabic nicknames. When I said Edward or he Dominique, it meant this was no time for jokes or indulgence.

We often talked about intellectual omnipotence. He found it hard to understand – I found it hard to explain – why I remained partially resistant to the method of *Culture and Imperialism*, though I thought it masterful. I once told him, 'That book lacks the other side of what it's denouncing. It lacks an element of impotence.' He looked at me in bemusement. This point of incomprehension marked a division between us that neither wanted to explore. Let us just say that Gramsci had more power over him than over me, Kafka over me rather than over him. Not to mention Cioran, with whom I joyfully, dangerously learned to laugh at anything that didn't fall apart after taking itself seriously.

Published fifteen years after *Orientalism*, *Culture and Imperialism* was the voluminous annexe to an original building that would have benefited, in my view, from a less massive addition. Edward's exceptional erudition, his formidable work of verifying and comparing associations certainly justified a reinforcement of his thesis, given the inexhaustible nature of the theme of colonial Empire in its many variations, internalised by so many western thinkers. So, the pages in *Culture and Imperialism* devoted to Verdi's *Aïda*, Kipling's *Kim* and Austen's *Mansfield Park* undoubtedly supplement the thinking on imperialism's capacity to infiltrate the imagination, outlined in *Orientalism*. What I regretted at the time, and regret still more on rereading it today, is that, having asserted his thesis with such force in *Orientalism*, Said did not opt for an addition that was more surprising and complex. More troubled. And, since he proclaimed counterpoint as his method, it would have been desirable – or so I feel – for him to use counterpoint not only within western orientalism – as he does in, for example, contrasting Camus' vision with that of Malraux and Gide – but within the two worlds that can be generally termed East and West. The place of mythology in Arab history written by Arabs, the very slow development of critical thinking and elements of self-censorship and hagiography also contribute to the extremely worrying distortion of the East's view of the East. And the East's view of the West. Hence my preference for a less defensive position, which did not confine itself to citing African or Arab authors with the courage to turn against the West's racist vision of their culture, but sought to explore the Arab East and a different form of blindness. The warped view of the Arab-Muslim world purveyed by so many western institutions and media sources should not make us forget that the transmission of knowledge by the schools, media and institutions of Arab countries is disastrous, notably concerning the history of racism among Arabs. Racism is a very weak word to describe thirteen centuries of slavery and African slave trading that humiliated, castrated and killed seventeen million people. How many universities, how many television programmes tell the public anything about this abomination? At the end of their years of schooling, do students know that the poet Al-Mutanabbi, whose work is taught and celebrated as among the greatest, calmly wrote that 'the lifetime of black slaves is limited by their stinking crotch and their teeth',[2] meaning that immortality is reserved for those who are not black? How many people know that the historian and philosopher Ibn Khaldun, whose pioneering work in history and sociology Edward rightly hails, simultaneously passed on the appalling vision of the African world that allowed horrific acts to be perpetrated with impunity? 'The Negro nations are, as a rule, submissive to slavery, because [Negroes] have little that is (essentially) human and possess attributes that are quite similar to those of dumb animals.'[3] The pursuit of his argument in the face of solid barrages of bad faith inevitably led its author down shortcuts and dead ends. In continuing and reinforcing the approach of *Orientalism*, *Culture and Imperialism* would have been more consistent if, taking History as its witness, it had concluded with the universal crisis in relations with the other, as discussed notably by Elias Canetti in *Crowds and Power*.[4] We should note, in passing, that Said does not cite Canetti in any of his books. Perhaps he was – understandably – annoyed by the essentialist aspects of Canetti's thought. But, aside from that pitfall – to which Nietzsche's genius was not immune either – which twentieth-century author better helps us

understand the mechanisms that create masses, set them against
one another and destroy alterity? Because, as Edward constantly
wrote, being the victim of domination does not in itself protect
against the danger of repeating history the other way round. The
Israeli government's deeply perverse approach to the Palestinians
is one example among many of the appalling fact that, just as being
a victim of racism is no protection against being racist, so suffering
does not prevent its victims from causing suffering. It is true that,
in the chapter 'American Ascendancy: The Public Space at War',
Said does not mince his words in discussing the 'Arab point of
view', in which he says the image of America is 'just as skewed'.[5] But,
reading this passage, we can clearly see that the crushing asymmetry of the power relations immediately drives Edward back to his
fight against American imperialism. His indictment is urgent,
convincing and particularly brave as, coming from both worlds at
once, he was comparatively alone in combating the ignorance of
the stronger side with such spirit and so many arguments.
However, *Culture and Imperialism* was published in 1993, two
years after the first Gulf war, when the Arab world had just
received the last of a long series of blows that had laid it low. Why?
Unlike Japan and India, and beyond the obvious consequences
of colonialism and imperialism, why had the immune system of
these cultures, these countries, become so weak as to be almost
gone? The West certainly bore a vast proportion of the blame, but,
as we say in Arabic, 'you can't clap with one hand only'. As long as
the Arabs haven't looked at themselves and examined their own
problem with otherness, as long as their conception of the precolonial past is confined to the good old days of Andalusia, they will
be cut off from their future. Said constantly alerted us to the
weaknesses of critical thinking in the Arab Middle East, and
the lack of dissident positions – with the evident exception of all
those who went against the grain and sometimes paid for it with
years of imprisonment. Nevertheless, most seem to take the view
that colonialism and imperialism exonerated them for their own
earlier crimes. Let us say that Edward's debt to Said made him

keener to give official status to his critique of the West than to
that of the East. The same was long true of me, on my own small
scale. It was also true of a considerable number of Arab Christians
linked to the West by culture, since Arabic was not their working
language, who then felt doubly responsible – I would even say
guilty. Just like Edward, the older brother of four sisters with
English-sounding given names out of Victorian novels – Jean,
Rosy, Grace and Joyce – who, in *Out of Place*, describes the unman-
ageable divorce between his given name and surname, I could not
get over the fact that my Syrian-Egyptian maternal grandfather
had changed his surname from Maqsoud[6] to Maksud, while my
Lebanese paternal grandfather had changed his given name Jamil
to Camille. The influence of Anglo-American imperialism on
Edward's branch of the family, and the French colonial influence
on mine, undoubtedly helped shape our political engagements
and the great complicity between us. For both of us the 'beginning' was a mistake to be remedied; the image of power, associated
with the father, was to be attacked. Our penchant for debate and
argument provided a screen for our unconscious motivations and,
for a long time, we kept our political struggle and our personal
histories separate. Edward largely dismantled this divide with the
introspective writing of *Out of Place*. It goes without saying that
the discovery that political activism depends in part on personal
history does not in any way invalidate the content of the cause.
But it does shed light on it. It is surely no coincidence that both of
us tirelessly, and at great cost – though on very different scales –
supported the Palestinian and secular Arab cause that others, who
might have been better armed, if only in terms of language, sometimes deserted with never a backward glance. If Edward had been
born into a Muslim anti-imperialist family and given an Arab
name, would he have put so much energy and effort into fighting
against imperialism and defending Arab culture? And, were it not
for my given name, my deficiencies in Arabic culture and the very
close relationship between my family and the French Mandate,
would I have started fighting, so young and with such zeal, against

the material and psychological effects of colonialism? In *The Genealogy of Morals*, Nietzsche writes, 'Have these genealogists of morals had even the remotest suspicion that, for example, the major moral concept *Schuld* (guilt) has its origin in the very material concept *Schulden* (debts)?'[7] Edward and I had debts of the same kind. They brought us closer intellectually, and shaped our shared conception of political morality and our need to weaken its grip by escaping into literature and music. In short, Said's work is a way of repaying those debts, with remarkable consistency and precision, and ultimately shedding them, or at least owing less. Given that in Arabic the letters *DIN*, differently emphasised, refer to both debt and religion – *al dayn* and *al din* – the next part of Nietzsche's argument is doubly striking: 'Punishment, as requital, evolved quite independently of any presupposition concerning freedom or non-freedom of the will.'[8] By extension, we can surely say that religion is the quintessential repayment, without proof or will, of a debt linking ignorance to guilt.

VII

It was during a conversation with André Green that I became
fully aware of the relationship between personal history and theoretical options. 'I have to say', he told me, 'that, rather than
surprise, I felt a certain sense of consistency when I read a piece in
Le Monde describing the wretched private life of Michel Foucault,
who used to go and have himself whipped in San Francisco's seedy
bars. "Discipline and punish"! . . . The denouncer of social structures that didn't make sense was himself a seeker of masochistic
pleasures.' When I asked whether that affected the credibility of
Foucault's work, Green replied, 'I would say something different. I
would say that I can't regard Foucault's sado-masochistic practices
as contingent, although they in no way detract from the solidity of
his work.'[1] In turn, I would say that I can't regard our 'orientalist'
origins – Arab American in Edward's case, French Arab in mine –
as contingent in relation to our political choices. This does not
detract from the internal consistency of those choices and,
crucially, does not alter the solidity of Said's work. Aside from the
determining factors of family that I have just described, his work
is very much in the tradition of the *Nahda* or Arab Renaissance.
Beginning in the mid-nineteenth century and still underway in
1914, this was a movement above and beyond religion, strongly
influenced by the intellectual input of Christian Arabs such as
Faris Shidyaq, Butrus al-Bustani, Francis Marrash, Jurji Zaydan
and many others. In using the word renaissance, I am aware that it
raises unresolved questions. Was it a new beginning or a return to

the source? This remains a matter of debate. I would add that dissidence in the Middle East – an assertion of the difference between a person's community of origin and their publicly stated political positions – has generally been more widespread in Christian Arab circles than among Muslims, notably in the twentieth century.

The father – biological father or substitute paternal figure – is where we all begin our more or less conscious negotiations with the notion of authority. The palette of possible reactions – which are not mutually exclusive – includes constructing the self through opposition or repetition and an investment that may be constructive or destructive. Or one could say that the absence of a father is still a father, in the way that, as Pessoa would say, the absence of God is still a God. Genet gave us a dazzling example of the conversion of this absence into individual omnipotence. The portraits of their respective fathers drawn by Conrad and Said are in striking contrast. At opposite extremes. Apollo is seen by his son as 'a man of great sensibilities; of exalted and dreamy temperament; with a terrible gift of irony and of gloomy disposition; withal of strong religious feeling, degenerating after the loss of his wife into mysticism touched with despair'.[2] Conrad's father wrote plays and poems, joined a popular literature group for the education of the peasants and began translating Victor Hugo's *La Légende des siècles*. His brother-in-law Thaddeus Bobrowski summed up his character in a letter to Conrad: 'Your father was an idealistic dreamer.'

Aged forty when his son Edward was born, Wadie Said was a Palestinian businessman, proud to be an American citizen and little interested in Palestine or Arab nationalism. He hated Jerusalem, saying it made him think of death. His portrait in *Out of Place* is that of a sober man with no literary leanings – unlike his wife. A man who was abrupt, humourless, focused on achieving full success in his field and little given to verbal expressions of affection. He is the opposite of Apollo the idealistic dreamer. At regular intervals, twice a month, he would send a typewritten letter to his son who, at the age of fifteen, had gone to study in the United States. He always signed it, 'Yours truly, W. A. Said'. Edward, who once complained to his mother about this paternal coldness, describes in a hilarious passage that he then received the following handwritten letter: 'Dear Edward, Your mother tells me that you don't like my typed letters to you but I am very busy as you can imagine. Anyway, here is a hand-written letter for you. Yours truly, W. A. Said.'[3] This 'sort of Dickensian father figure, despotic when angered, benevolent when not'[4] was as uninterested in thinking or talking about the past as his son would later be obsessed by doing so. The passages on his mother, a central figure in his life, suggest that she actively worked to distance Edward from his father, in order to create an exclusive relationship with her only son, born shortly after the death of an older brother. She also saw to it that Edward's relationship with his four sisters, who are largely absent from his autobiography, passed or did not pass through her.

> My relationship to my two older sisters, Jean and Rosy, was usually a prickly, adversarial one, and I felt we slowly lost the habit of intimacy and even of accommodation with each another.
>
> To her dying day my mother was a bilateralist; that is, she encouraged us to deal with each other through her . . . only one of us could be favored at a time.[5]

Of course, his relationships with his sisters – which he often talked about – varied from one to the next, but were generally characterised by a contradictory mix of need and love, lack of communication and frustration. Without really accepting it, Edward maintained the distance between them. We shall necessarily come back to his mother, Hilda Said, particularly since couples – his parents and by extension couples in themselves – are central to Edward's comparative thinking. Whether in relation to politics (Israel and Palestine, East and West), history (North and

South), philosophy (the dialogue between Foucault and Foucault in *The Archaeology of Knowledge*), literature (Conrad and his double) or music (*Così fan tutte* in which, through two pairs of lovers, 'human identity is shown to be as protean, unstable and undifferentiated as anything'),[6] Edward was always negotiating the more or less conflicted, paradoxical relations between two divided, coexisting extremes – between an insoluble, inevitable couple, with no way out but the movement that relays meaning from one extreme to the other.

During the First World War, Wadie Said served in the American Expeditionary Force, in which he was exposed to the rigours of Camp Gordon,[7] where 'his reaction to a battery of inoculations meant that he spent most of basic training ill and in bed'.[8]

> Whatever the actual historical facts were, my father came to represent a devastating combination of power and authority, rationalistic discipline and repressed emotions; and all this, I later realized, has impinged on me my whole life, with some good, but also some inhibiting and even debilitating effects.[9]

We cannot read Said's work or follow the development of his thought, his gradual conquest of independence, the effort and price this required of him, without considering his relationship with his parents. Underpinning his rebellion against the superiority with which the West views the East – which gave rise to *Orientalism* – were two processes of liberation: on the one hand, liberation from a father who sided with the stronger power (America) and – far more complex and difficult to express – a possessive, volatile mother; on the other, at the collective level, the liberation of peoples abused by dominant powers. His journey took him in the opposite direction to that of the orphan Conrad, who wrote in 1917: 'It lies on me to confess at last, and this is as good a place for it as another, that I have been all my life – all my two lives – the spoiled adopted child of Great Britain and even of

the Empire; for it was Australia that gave me my first command.'[10]
Conrad was seeking to repay what Green calls 'the debt' – his
father's revolutionary lack of awareness – by winning the battle
against the threat of dying at sea.

> Captain Korzeniowski's first command was a descent into
> hell . . . It was the evidence Conrad was waiting for to prove his
> worth, to demonstrate his capacity to endure and cede nothing
> to death, to retain his crew's trust and to bring them back
> to land . . . He would no longer need the perils of the sea to
> compensate for his father's failings . . . Writing would be a new
> form of reparation. Henceforth Conrad would have to struggle
> only with himself.[11]

It would be an understatement to say that the relationships
between Conrad and Said and their countries of adoption were
asymmetrical. They were polar opposites. Conrad was full of gratitude for his new family, which necessarily included the Empire,
but this did not lead him to abandon his pessimistic intelligence
and critical ferocity towards human beings, regardless of their
origins among imperialist or subject peoples. Said acknowledged
that, in material and moral terms, his father had given him the
means to construct himself; the son was angry with the father for
having bullied and repressed him and, above all, for having made
him live in 'foreign' surroundings in an Arab country. For having
sided with Empire. In *Out of Place* he writes,

> Until 1967 I succeeded in mentally dividing US support for
> Israel from the fact of my being an American pursuing a career
> there and having Jewish friends and colleagues. The remote-
> ness of the Palestine I grew up in, my family's silence over its
> role, and then its long disappearance from our lives, my moth-
> er's open discomfort with the subject and later aggressive
> dislike of both Palestine and politics, my lack of contact
> with Palestinians during the eleven years of my American

education: all this allowed me to live my early American life at a great distance from the Palestine of remote memory, unresolved sorrow, and uncomprehending anger.[12]

Said's 'debt' was the opposite of Conrad's. It was to those subjected to Empire that he owed reparations for his father's failing and, more broadly, his family context. In *Out of Place*, he describes 'a family determined to make itself into a mock little European group despite the Egyptian and Arab surroundings that are only hinted at as an occasional camel, gardener, servant, palm tree, pyramid, or tarbushed chauffeur is briefly caught by the camera's otherwise single-minded focus on the children and assorted relatives.'[13] What better illustration of orientalism could he use to help us understand his combat against it? But Conrad and Said had another dominant trait in common, and that was irony. It is irony that provided the ground on which Edward encountered his own world and its other side in that of Conrad, and which enabled him to oppose the ideas of his father and mother, without abandoning the weapons of critical thinking that he owed to his western education. Here, we see the extreme complexity, ambivalence and flexibility of his thinking. He was not seeking to abandon anything, but rather, through constant effort, to reconcile all that he had gained with all that he rejected, comfort with separation. His was a world of duality. So much so that, more than once, his portrait of Conrad contains his own. We see this when he describes 'Conrad's radical uncertainty about himself and also the tension he so often felt between opposed positions on any given matter',[14] and in his choice of quotation from Conrad's letter to his agent J B Pinker: 'I don't resemble anybody . . . There is nothing in me but a turn of mind which, whether valuable or worthless, cannot be imitated.'[15] This turn of mind that cannot be imitated is also what Said endlessly sought and embodied. Marlow, Nostromo, Decoud, Lord Jim and many others among Conrad's characters fuelled Edward's imagination at those points where his strictly political positions could not, in themselves, satisfy his emotions. In October 1891, Conrad wrote to his aunt, 'Good heavens, could I be a Punch? The Punch of my childhood, you know – his spine broken in two, his nose on the floor between his feet, his legs and arms flung out stiffly in that attitude of deep despair, so pathetically droll, of dolls tossed in a corner.'[16] Reading this, one is reminded of that other transformation of the self, imagined by Said to escape his father's merciless physical surveillance:

> One of my recurrent fantasies, the subject of a school essay I wrote when I was twelve, was to be a book, whose fate I took to be happily free of unwelcome changes, distortions of its shape, criticism of its looks; print for me was made up of a rare combination of expression in its style and contents, absolute rigidity, and integrity in its looks. Passed from hand to hand, place to place, time to time, I could remain my own true self (as a book), despite being thrown out of a car and lost in a back drawer.[17]

Why 'thrown out of a car'? Why this metaphor? This is perhaps the moment to consider an event in Edward's life that has not been elucidated. I am stunned that it did not bring me up short on my first reading. It was not until fifteen years after his death, rereading, pencil in hand, that I recognised the importance of something that was there in black and white at the very end of his autobiography. This was a serious car accident that happened in Switzerland. Edward was then aged twenty-two. In the sentence preceding the account of the collision, he describes the almost hypnotic power of his bond with his mother: 'I still regarded her as my point of reference, mostly in ways that I neither fully apprehended nor concretely understood.' Then he relates,

> In the summer of 1958, while driving in Switzerland, I had a horrendously bloody, head-on collision with a motorcyclist; he was killed and I was badly hurt. I can still recall with a jolt that awesomely loud and terrifyingly all-encompassing sound of the

actual collision, which knocked me unconscious, and the very moment I awakened on the grass with a priest bending over me trying to administer the last rites. A moment later, after pushing away the intrusive cleric, with infallible instinct I knew I had to call my mother, who at that very moment was in Lebanon, with the rest of my family. She was the first person to whom I needed to tell my story, which I did the moment the ambulance delivered me to the Fribourg hospital. That feeling I had of both beginning and ending with my mother, of her sustaining presence and, I imagined, infinite capacity for cherishing me, softly, imperceptibly, underwrote my life for years and years.[18]

Why is Edward at once so clear and so allusive in the story of this accident that proved fatal to the motorcyclist? What happened? Having, throughout his work – and notably in *Out of Place* – shown such scrupulous concern for detail and precision, for the first time he leaves his reader guessing. Having followed Conrad in staying a step ahead of his reader every time there was a need to clarify or justify the why and how of his writings, why, in this particular case, did he opt for a version that does not set out the facts, with no before and after? The dead motorcyclist is anonymous. He has no age, no story.[19] The two themes that haunt Said's work, 'the beginning and the end', are here given to the mother, absorbed by her. Christian guilt, embodied by the priest, is sent packing and barely alluded to. Why is no light shed on this accident? We might, of course, assume that he was not in the wrong, since it seems there was no prosecution. We might also think, that, being in shock, he had every reason to lose his memory of what actually happened. But we cannot skip over the very likely consequences of this death for his psychological life, which already bore the heavy stamp of guilt, due to his education. 'He was killed and I was badly hurt' is all he says. How can we not imagine the trauma concealed within these eight words from a man who could be crushed by a sense of having done wrong with far less cause? How, moreover, can we not link this block, this blank, to the context into which he inserts this story – his relationship with his mother? A close reading of *Out of Place* leaves no doubt. It was his mother, the 'point of reference' that he never managed to 'fully apprehend', who turned her son's guilt on and off. It was she who burdened him and, temporarily, exonerated him. Did she burden him, exonerate him, or both, when she came to see him in Switzerland? What is clear from *Out of Place* is that her approval was never given once and for all, but had constantly to be won anew.

> She had the most deep-seated and unresolved ambivalence toward the world, and me, I have ever known . . . Between my mother's empowering, sunlike smile and her cold scowl or her sustained frowning dismissiveness, I existed as a child both fortunate and hopelessly miserable, neither completely one nor the other.[20]

This movement, this constant back and forth, is not unrelated to that of Said's thought and writing. His mobility and extreme, never-satisfied rigour. The dual relationship of seduction and warning that he maintains with his reader, in which the suspense of a potential change of direction becomes an almost vital, Nietzschean aspect of his thought, the one that enabled him to make his arguments so nuanced and, simultaneously, exposed them to misunderstanding. His work, his political writings – notably *Orientalism* – can be read in many different ways. There is a reading that foregrounds subtlety, and another that hides it in favour of caricature. Reading him properly means dealing, as he did, with both registers at once, and allowing oneself the same right to identify the difference between paradox and contradiction. As Gilles Deleuze wrote, paradox displays 'the element that cannot be totalised within a common element'.[21]

Bearing in mind that his book *Beginnings* is subtitled *Intention and Method*, we might say that Edward's 'intention' is strongly determined by the figure of his father, taking the form of a challenge to knowledge and vertical power – imperialism – and that his 'method' is more influenced by his mother, in constant returns to foundations that must always be rediscovered, remade. More than his father Wadie, it was his mother Hilda who dominated his emotions, praising then hurting him, issuing permission followed by prohibition, adoring then endangering him, without his ever really knowing the criteria to which he should attribute any of these sudden changes. In this paragraph on the 'mother–accident–mother' it seems as though Edward's moral rigour dictated that he could not end his memoirs without describing this serious accident, and that his mother gave him the escape route that spared him the duty to decipher or take on its meaning with anyone but her. I open this parenthesis after some hesitation, because it seems to me to elucidate several points in relation to Edward and his work. It provides a possible additional explanation of the omnipresence of guilt and shame in his depiction of himself and the world, as in the work of Conrad. How can we know, other than hypothetically, the consequences of this event in Switzerland for the rest of his career? In its secrecy, it might be compared to the famous episode in Marseille, which marked the life of the young Conrad at the very similar age of twenty-one. In the winter of 1878, Conrad's uncle Bobrowski received a telegram: 'Conrad wounded, send money – come.' The uncle rushed to Marseille, tried to find out what had happened and paid some debts. At the time, and in later years, Conrad strove to persuade his friends and family that his injury was due to a duel over a woman. It was only in 1957 – through a letter to his father's friend Stephen Buszczynski – that the truth came out. Conrad had invited Flecht, his creditor – for gambling debts – to have tea and had probably staged a failed suicide attempt just before his arrival. One thing is certain: no vital organs were affected, and he made sure that a friend, called by Flecht, arrived in time. This put an end to the story of a duel. According to Green,

During this period Conrad was involved in Carlist political activities and even traded in arms. This entire phase of chaotic, sometimes dangerous living came to an end with a second change of direction. Just as he had turned his back on Poland and land in general, he made a new volte-face, broke his ties with France and headed for England – despite knowing almost nothing of its language – and the British navy. I would tend to interpret this second about-turn as a choice of discipline – supervision – that had the approval of his uncle, and indeed of requital linked to a desire to start a new life conforming to British values, which in him coincided with the values of seamen.'[22]

There are no obvious comparisons here between Conrad and Said, except for one, not insignificant, thing: a certain sense of 'redemption'. In the light of what happened in Switzerland, Edward's 'volte-face' on the question of his identity can also be seen as a form of recompense. As a certain 'choice of discipline – supervision' linked to rebellion against the established family order. In 1967, the year of the Six-Day War and his divorce from his first wife Maire Jaanus, Said experienced an awakening, and with it a change of direction. He returned to his Arab roots and took on the twin tasks of defending the Palestinian people and attacking the western clichés that trapped and distorted views of the East, passed on by his parents within the family. One thing is certain: after the accident, he settled down to write his thesis on Conrad, who became his lifelong travelling companion or, more precisely, 'secret sharer'. 'Conrad, Said's "secret companion"' was the title I gave to a conference paper given a year after his death,[23] without realising, at the time, the full extent of my intuition. 'Write about me and Conrad one day', Edward said to me. It's an understatement to say that I am now missing a reader, that I would have liked to share with him my exploration of his unconscious – and my own at the same time. So, what is the story of *The Secret Sharer*?

The narrator has recently been appointed captain of a ship with a crew who, unlike him, are highly experienced. Alone on deck, having sent his sailors below to sleep, he sees the masts of an approaching ship, the *Sephora*, from which a man jumps into the sea and swims towards him. The rope ladder is still down and the captain invites the man aboard. Secrecy is established at once. The captain gives the man clothes, 'a sleeping suit of the same gray-stripe pattern as the one I was wearing, and [he] followed me like my double on the poop.'[24] He hides the man, Leggatt, in his cabin. The clandestine visitor soon proves to be the narrator's double. 'I've killed a man', says the double. This is the start of a disturbing relationship between the narrator and his double, between Conrad and Conrad. The guilty man explains why he committed murder – he wanted to punish a sailor who was refusing to do his duty. He grabbed him by the throat and, with a storm raging, things ended badly. In telling his story, Leggatt refers several times to his father, a pastor who, unlike Conrad, could never have understood his son's motivations. We are reminded here of the priest bending over Edward after he was thrown out of the car.[25] The men of the *Sephora* soon come looking for the fugitive. The captain of the *Sephora* gives his version of events, which Conrad does not pass on to the reader. According to Green, 'The result is that the young captain, the secret companion's double, cannot help identifying with him even more.' 'It's a great satisfaction to have got somebody to understand', says Leggatt. When, on the pretext of trying to catch the off-shore breeze, the captain helps Leggatt to leave his ship, 'Our hands met gropingly, lingered united in a steady, motionless clasp for a second.' In this 'immedi-ate recognition, this community of soul', Green sees 'the final return of the past before the doors of the future are opened'. A little later he says, 'In reality it is not Leggatt's person that is the object of singular attraction, but what he represents – a killer to be killed, another self to be made to disappear.' What would Edward say if he could read these words as I write them? I don't know. His curiosity being what it was – much greater than his satisfaction in knowing what he knew – and his personal and intellectual familiarity with Freudian analysis having grown over the years, I like to think he would have said, with his irresistible smile tinged with irony, 'Bravo D.' Be that as it may, I think he would have agreed with Green's conclusion, which applies as much to Said's morality as to Conrad's. It is also the subject of my essay: 'This morality is what dictates the duty to understand. Understanding means taking a step back, accepting the other as another self, and it is this benefit that the double wants from the man who listens to him. He hopes not to be saved, but to be understood.'[26]

VIII

Said's thesis on Conrad was first published in 1966. The jacket copy of a new edition published in 2008 presented it as a book in which 'Edward W. Said locates Joseph Conrad's fear of personal disintegration in his constant re-narration of the past.'[1] The same could be said of Said. His eclecticism, his dual culture, his eccentricity and above all his fear of finitude constantly threaten his work with collapse, which he combats through perpetual recapitulation, injecting the past into his ideas as they leave it behind. It is no coincidence that the eighteenth century, embodied by Swift, Vico and Rousseau, is never far away whenever Said joins authors of his own time like Foucault, Deleuze and Jacques Derrida, on the path of deconstruction towards a future that is hard to see. In a chapter on 'The Novel as Beginning Intention', Said wrote of *Nostromo*:

> Nearly everyone in the novel seems extremely anxious about both keeping and leaving a personal 'record' of his thoughts and action. This anxiety seems to be based upon an extraordinary preoccupation with the past, as if the past, left to itself, given only ordinary attention and no official recording, were somehow unthinkable and without sufficient authority.[2]

This anxiety is Said's own. What is 'the past left to itself' if not untamed territory, more jungle than garden, more natural than human? And what is this jungle that at once drew and frightened both Conrad and Said, if not the heart of darkness? The mystery of origins. And also that part of the self that is beyond control – the unconscious. Not forgetting that Said's father precisely did leave 'the past to itself'. One through fiction, the other through essays, these two exiled authors, whose mother tongue was not English, built a rampart against the void in the form of a cultivated, domesticated past. A past previously untouched by human hands; a past brought out of limbo, identified, analysed and understood. This is no doubt one of the many reasons why Conrad loathed Dostoevsky and Said took a cautious, economical approach to the author of *The Possessed*, for whom garden and jungle, origins and beginnings, grew wild together within one person. Although Dostoevsky is discussed in *Beginnings*, he is not mentioned in the index – deliberate omission or Freudian slip? Said's discussion of *The Possessed* focuses on its author's relationship to the past.

> This discontinuity feeds our ever-increasing suspicion of a narrator anxious to make outrageous events conform to the seeming order of his narrative. Our suspicion is aroused from the novel's very opening, so strongly, in fact, that we soon consider the narrator himself as much a Quixote as we do Stepan Trofimovich. For what is one to make of a reporter whose introductory account of a character is as full of purposeful vagueness as that character himself? . . . The hedgings, the doubts, the second- and third-hand reports, the ambiguous passive constructions, the leaps in argument – all are part of a textual fabric badly concealing its radical internal discontinuity as well as its disjunctive relations with reality. Furthermore, every human relationship in the novel seems to lack connection and defy consummation: marriages, in other words, are either ended or unrecognized, whether in the legal state or outside it. Consequently the relations between men and women, as well as those between parents and children, are uniformly skewed.[3]

Later, in relation to Stavrogin's confession, Said concludes his analysis as follows:

> One of the points of this difficult scene, I think, is that writing and psychology conspire to overwhelm any morality or ethic based upon a common sense understanding of consequence. Whereas such understanding stipulates that the consequence of a confessed crime is absolution for the believer as well as punishment, Tihon (whom Stavrogin calls a 'cursed psychologist') argues that so complex are the mind and its refractions in writing that one cannot expect to find any consecutive sense in them at all.[4]

This lack of clear information, and the impossibility of evaluating and identifying the levels of guilt, repentance and punishment, lead Said to conclude: 'Dostoevsky's technique is to make text, sequential time and understanding, the biological order of human genealogy all, in his novel, totally discontinuous elements.' Dostoevsky's sleight of hand has brought us back to the question that haunts all of Said's work: when in time can the beginning, the end and the repetition be located? Manifestly more at ease with the intellectual approach of discontinuity and deconstruction in the style of Foucault and Derrida, than with its emotional and psychological application, Said is more threatened by Dostoevsky's world than by Conrad's. Dostoevsky destabilises and disarms him, whereas Conrad provides him with a clock and a context in which to reconcile anxiety and ethics, his two preoccupations. Anxiety absorbs guilt, ethics offers him a way out which, though insufficient, has the great merit of calming anxiety by offering a morality founded on will, character and action – the morality of 'doing what you have to do'. In other words, steering the ship to port, against all diabolical temptations and notably money and women. There is nothing of this in Dostoevsky, for whom internal and external storms are intertwined, will has little power against instinct, reason is infiltrated by madness and the shadow of God is everywhere, including within characters who are unbelievers. Here lies the gulf between the worlds of these two novelists. God and madness haunt Dostoevsky's world but are absent from that of Conrad who, although he too exists in an atmosphere of torment, nerves and guilt, invents a form of order founded on morality, whereas Dostoevsky follows chaos through the soul's every fold and wrinkle. In the late 1970s, through my friendship with Cioran, who had a passion for Dostoevsky and talked about him a great deal, I came to understand the latter's unique, highly revealing power of attraction or repulsion for a great many authors, including those to whom he could least be compared. Why did Freud, who regarded Dostoevsky as the greatest of all novelists, feel such great antipathy for him? The answer does not – or not only – lie in Dostoevsky's anti-Semitism, but perhaps also in his masochism and amorality, recompensed in extremis by Christian redemption. Why was Nietzsche, who proclaimed the death of God and Christianity, enchanted by the work of Dostoevsky? Why did Genet, with all his preoccupation with form, overt rejection of Christianity and an approach to human beings that was more theatrical than realist, regard Dostoevsky as the most brilliant of novelists? Why did Cioran, who told me he dreamed of writing his last book on the writer who tested the nerve of believers and unbelievers alike, not manage to do so? Whenever Edward and I discussed Dostoevsky, it was only in comparison to Tolstoy. We would always reach the same point: Edward identified more with Tolstoy and I with Dostoevsky – in those days, at least. The figure of the double, as central to Dostoevsky as to Conrad and Said, is where the divergence between their ways of seeing human beings becomes clear. For Conrad and Said, the double is a threatening but familiar companion who espouses the contours of consciousness the same way a shadow follows those of the body. For Dostoevsky, the double is not an interlocutor but an other, whose similarity has the power to undo all equilibrium. In the novella *The Double*, Dostoevsky portrays a rival brother who unleashes and foments war and madness within the human being. He is not a close friend, nor even another self like Leggatt, but a mortal enemy. He is absolute danger, the threat of losing one's reason. This sheds some light on the similarity between Freud, Nietzsche and the author of *The Brothers Karamazov*, for whom a wind stronger than the self blows within the self – a wind with which consciousness alone cannot negotiate. The equivalent of the 'id' in Freudian terms. This is what Golyadkin Junior is made of; he turns against Golyadkin Senior, traps him, takes his money, reduces him to ridicule and finally to the asylum. In the end the original becomes the plaything of the copy, in contrast to Leggatt, who establishes a connection between the captain and himself, like a musical legato. Dostoevsky's double represents the destruction of connection, in a metaphysical context. A kind of devil in God's head.

The relationship Said maintained with both Conrad and Dostoevsky – secure in the timescale of the former, overwhelmed in the timescale of the latter – sheds light on a remembered scene that made an impression on me. It was the early 1980s. Edward and I were walking among the ruins of the Forum in Rome. After a while, he began to feel ill. At first, I thought he was just tired and suggested he should sit down. He hesitated, walked forward, then flopped down on the base of a column. Bent double, head in his hands, he told me he was experiencing a terrible crisis. He couldn't speak, he was very pale, he needed to be alone. I walked a little way away, out of his field of vision, and waited. I grew more and more worried. How long did this scene go on for? I don't remember. What I do remember is that later he described it as 'a total collapse'. 'It was the worst nightmare', he told me, 'The feeling that I no longer belonged to myself, of no longer connecting, of falling apart and disintegrating'. I didn't know what to say, how to understand it. The next day, his anxiety had subsided and, egotistically, I attributed this scene to our relationship. To the fear of betraying, of not being able to choose or decide. It is only now, with hindsight – focusing on him – that I see a link between this panic attack and the timescale of the ruins. Perhaps that day he suddenly fell victim to the realisation of his fear, which was also the fear he saw in Conrad. The fear of collapse that they both dealt with by turning to the past. The past on the human scale of recent centuries and not the crushing scale of Antiquity. Perhaps the distinction between origins and beginnings, which underpinned his equilibrium, had been shaken when he found himself surrounded by ruins, prey to 'a past left to itself'. Ultimately, it was as though the time in which he lived, thought, loved and wrote had given way to the pressure from an earlier, untameable time, just as a floor will give way under weight. His sense of the 'ground opening up beneath his feet' was surely linked to the overturning of the present time by the infinitely remote, and yet so concretely present time of Roman Antiquity. Unless captured and tamed in a poem by Cavafy, as light is tamed by blinds, Roman Antiquity was not a period in which Said could move freely. I may be wrong, I may be right, who can tell? What is certain, from the account he gave the next day, is that in that time and place he fell prey to another self who did not wish him well. This is the other that Conrad brings safe and sound to shore in *The Secret Sharer*, whereas, in *The Double*, Dostoevsky lets him destroy everything.

IX

Shortly before his death, I surprised and, I think, convinced Edward by telling him that his father's initial inserted between Edward and Said, his *W*, was also his 'double you'. Edward double you Said. In *Out of Place* he writes, 'At the age of five or six . . . I regularly referred to myself not as "me" but as "you". "Mummy doesn't love you, naughty boy," she would say, and I would respond, in half-plaintive echoing, half-defiant assertion, "Mummy doesn't love you, but Auntie Melia loves you."' *You* instead of *me*. Is it pure coincidence that the letter *W* separates Theodor from Adorno, who also constantly had to negotiate between his identity as a Jew and a Christian, between Germany and America, his father – Wiesengrund – and the mother whose surname he adopted? Wadie was also the name Edward gave his son. So that his concern with affiliation rather than filiation was not always that clear. Whether or not we are in exile, tradition still has power in our cultures. For Edward, rebellion and transgression in relation to the father, which was apparent in his relationship to power, never crossed certain bounds at the personal level. His fight against power and the paternal figure took the form of a radical expression of disagreement, rather than deliberate all-out rejection and separation. And with good reason. Where his father was concerned, he never stopped feeling an indefinable mixture of fear and gratitude, uneasiness and pique, disappointment and admiration.

After we got back together in 1993, Edward would often tell me, 'I'm a dying man'. Aside from the need to share his anxiety, I think he felt that he was postponing death by making room for it. For more than a decade, it waited. As it had for his father, who was diagnosed with cancer in the 1950s, Edward's death took ten years. The pages he wrote about this imminent yet constantly postponed threat are among the subtlest in his autobiography. They convey the humour and affection afforded by hindsight towards the man who had so seriously intimidated him as a child.

> During the summer of 1961 he seemed to have died about half a dozen times. On those occasions we would leave him at about eight at night and be awakened in Dhour by a phone call at three the next morning: 'Come immediately,' a voice would say, 'he's very near the end'. We would bundle ourselves in a taxi and arrive at the hospital near dawn to find him in shock or in a coma. He seemed to have attracted every complication imaginable. First it was a murderous urinary tract infection; then he would miraculously recover, only to fall to a massive stomach haemorrhage. Then two days later he'd be sitting up being shaved by the little barber and chatting away.... Two days later, another four o'clock phone call, and this time when I arrived I'd hear a doctor say that for four minutes my father had been clinically dead ... For a week he lingered between extinction and a restless, half-conscious state.
>
> Two days more of this and once again he'd be being shaved as if nothing had happened.[1]

Throughout the month of August 1961, the same scenario was repeated, and grew more serious – if 'more serious' has any meaning in such a context. Edward was unsure whether to stay or fly home for a medical consultation he had deferred three times. His remorseless anxiety was fuelled by an impossible choice: Should he miss his father's death or endanger his own future? This figure of death that arrives and waits – sometimes tragically, sometimes amusingly – reappeared in his thought, his writing and also at the end of his own life. In all kinds of ways, Edward was always returning after having left, leaving before he had left and not leaving at all. His relationship to watches merits an essay in itself. Of his father he says, 'The gravity of his illness acted as an announcement of my father's and my own mortality and at the same time signalled to me that the Middle Eastern domain he had carved out for us as a home, a shelter, an abode of sorts, with its main points tied to Cairo, Dhour, and Palestine, was similarly threatened with discontinuity and evanescence.'[2] It is no coincidence that Edward's narrative simultaneously discusses the half-imperturbable, half-dying father and a first great love that he often spoke of in our conversations. She was called Eva, like his mother's cousin, the wife of Charles Malik. I draw attention to this shared name because he unknowingly repeats the same information twice on the same page: 'He was . . . the husband of my mother's first cousin Eva . . . He was married to Eva, my mother's first cousin.'[3] For a while, the Maliks embodied a kind of ideal, an alternative parental couple. Charles Malik was a diplomat and man of letters, who strongly influenced Said with his culture and charisma. But, here again, there was also ambivalence, which led to extreme political disappointment when 'Uncle Charles' changed sides. 'He began his public career during the late 1940s as an Arab spokesman for Palestine at the UN, but concluded it as the anti-Palestinian architect of the Christian alliance with Israel during the Lebanese Civil War.'[4] When Edward arrived in the United States for the first time, Charles and Eva were objects of fascination for him; very different from his own family, they combined luxury with political engagement. In Washington, 'Eva came by in her husband's black ambassadorial limousine almost immediately and, brooking no dissent, pried us and our lordly array of luggage out of the hotel and into the nicely comfortable chancellory.'[5] The discussions Edward had down the years with the haughty, brilliant and confident Charles Malik left their traces. Malik's alignment with his faith community opened the young Said's eyes to a trap that he was determined to avoid at all costs. 'I have always felt the priority of intellectual, rather than national or tribal, consciousness, no matter how solitary that made one,' he writes towards the end of *Out of Place*.[6] Edward's Eva was a few years his senior. He was twenty, she twenty-seven. Her religious background was Greek Orthodox, she was a French speaker and had a rather casual lifestyle. Edward's father, Wadie, on the one hand, conveyed his disapproval directly, without recourse to subtlety. His mother, on the other, remained true to her own methods, oscillating between incomprehension and reprisals. 'Her love for me meant that she saw any other emotional attachment as a diminishment of her hold over me.'[7] The question of marriage emerged when Edward graduated from Princeton in 1957. Eva was then living in Alexandria with her widowed sister. 'Our physical relationship remained passionate but unconsummated because we both had the notion that once we had crossed that line we would to all intents be a married couple.'[8] When Edward failed to make up his mind, Eva went to Cairo to see Hilda Said and seek to obtain her approval. It is easy to imagine what happened next. 'Let me be perfectly honest with you', said Edward's mother. 'You're a wonderful person with a great deal to offer. The problem isn't you, it's Edward. You're much better than he is.'[9] The issue of finance arose and Eva fought back, objecting that she had more than enough money for both of them. Hilda Said chose to ignore this. 'Why throw away your future on someone as unstable as he? Take my advice, Eva, you can do much better than that.'[10] The narcissistic wound caused by this fearsome power of manipulation, combined with his immense attachment to his mother, would never close.

> Any attempts to dislodge her sense of deterministic certitude about me was impossible. It was not so much her clemency I wanted, but for her to admit that I might have changed, and to modify her views held with such a dispiriting combination of serene confidence and unassailable cheerfulness, as if her son were fixed forever in his inventory of vices and virtues of whom she had been the first, and certainly the most authoritative, chronicler.[11]

It was Hilda who, a few weeks later, informed her son of Eva's engagement to her cousin, showing him the Egyptian daily paper *al-Ahram*, in which the news was announced. During his chaste relationship with Eva, Edward says in *Out of Place* that he was having a fully sexual relationship with another woman in the United States. Beyond Said himself, this dual emotional, sexual and cultural life tells us much about the way that the imagination can be pulled back and forth between tradition and modernity, dependency and autonomy and perhaps also East and West. It is a distillation of so many love affairs experienced in the same and subsequent periods within the more or less cosmopolitan bourgeoisie of the Middle East. People were torn between tradition and the strength of family structures on the one hand, and freedom and anti-conformism acquired through books and travel on the other, in ways that are hard for westerners of comparable generations and social milieus to imagine. Shortly after Edward's death, I had a dream whose every detail remains etched in my memory. I am holding a child in my arms and am filled with feelings of love and tenderness. It is Edward as a little boy. A woman comes towards us carrying a small child. This child is holding a stick and threatening to hit my child. I look into its face. This other child is also Edward. And the woman is his mother. I wonder, how can I defend Edward against Edward? And I wake up with a start. This dream freed me from some of my remorse at not having done better while he was alive. Beneath the happiness of possibilities lay an impossible equation. When I first met Edward, he told her about us. She took a perverse pleasure in drawing power from her knowledge. Ultimately the main role was hers. I was shocked to learn that the little gold chain he had given me when he passed through Paris had been chosen by her in Beirut. When things became more serious, to the point where he found himself – as in the past – torn apart by an impossible choice, she intervened and bluntly settled the question. The time for indulgence was past. Pleading for a return to the way things were before, she was once again his arbiter and centre. Not that Edward lacked willpower. He had more than enough of that. But he was wounded in the place where the self is anchored through its image in the eyes of the other. That place was never secure. Between his mother's ambivalence and his father's harsh rigour, it is not certain that the latter was the harder to overcome.

In Edward's relationship to the father, God emerges more or less unscathed. Neither alive nor dead. He is declared absent by Edward, as by Conrad, whereas he is proclaimed non-existent by Sartre. Maybe an atheist, maybe not, Edward dispensed himself from the need to delve into the mystery, confining himself to the notion of secularism, which returns in his writing as often as atheism in the work of Sartre. Neither Said nor Conrad envisaged any help from God. 'It's not prayer that will save the ship', wrote André Green, 'but a cool head, lucidity, skill and solidarity between men, all simply human qualities.'[12]

Nor was it prayer, still less religion, to which Said looked to save Palestine. For both Said and Conrad, everything depended on the mind, in Coleridge's sense of 'a repetition in the finite mind of the eternal act of creation in the infinite I AM'.[13] 'From a reflective, historical standpoint, all human things (or institutions) are, from the beginning, created by the mind, *mind* understood as that which can begin intentionally to act in the world of men.'[14] Let us say that Edward positions himself halfway between Vico and Sartre. For Vico, 'God succeeds in influencing nature, whereas man succeeds only in influencing himself'.[15] For Sartre, 'man first of all exists, encounters himself, surges up in the world . . . he is nothing. He will not be anything until later, and then he will be what he makes of himself. Thus there is no human nature, because there is no God to have a conception of it.'[16] Edward does not decide. For him the question is not so much whether existence precedes essence, as to identify the previous existences on which existences are founded and repeat themselves in the present. He is unswervingly aligned with history. Vico offers the context he needs for his choice, and gives it legitimacy. He spares Said the question of origins by taking responsibility for God. To the extent that, for Vico, human will is exerted beyond the terrain of divine will, he provides Said with an argument that makes it possible to understand human beings in human terms and, at the same time, to leave God's business to God. In terms of method – management of anxiety and absence – it's a luxury. Since divine will does not intervene in human will, the word 'authority' – central in Said's work as in Vico's – is released from the determinism that usually goes hand in hand with religion or excessive faith in science. Said links *The New Science*'s notion of authority to the *autodidact*, a status Vico claimed for himself in his autobiography and which Said also adopted, in subjective rather than academic terms. Eccentricity being one of the most frequently used words – alongside hybridity and originality – in Said's political, literary and musical readings of works of human art. Of all Said's father figures, Vico is the most *senior* in both the proper and figurative senses. He gives Said permission. Hence this quotation from Vico near the end of *Beginnings*: 'human authority, in the full philosophical sense of the phrase, "is the property of human nature which not even God can take from man without destroying him . . . This authority is the free use of the will, the intellect, on the other hand, being a passive power subject to truth".'[17] This is how, through Vico, Said bound himself to human beings and to morality, and freed himself from God. This is how he used fundamentally secular language without offending believers, including, perhaps unconsciously, his own family. This is also how he began his own beginning and summed up his adherence to Vico's vision:

> The theory argues that just as in geometry one can posit a hypothetical beginning point from which lines can be extended (the point remaining a postulate, but one which is valid because all lines are divisible into infinitesimal indivisible points), so too in metaphysical terms one can posit a beginning point which is neither entirely mind (or abstraction) nor matter (concreteness). The so-called metaphysical point then becomes conation – what in this book I have been calling beginning

intentions – which in history is human will, understood both temporally and absolutely.[18]

In reality, Said's entire oeuvre rests on this decisive, sophisticated, more or less acknowledged moment of metaphysical negotiation: he profits from the no man's land established by Vico between God and men to attribute to Vico his observation of the crushing superiority of divine will over human will (this formal concession costs nothing, it doesn't require faith) in exchange for the autonomy of a human will that is aware of its limits. On this basis, he can *mineralise* the beginning, bringing it out of the thick wrapping of fog conceded to God. He can begin. *Beginnings* is the book on which Said grounds his legitimacy as an author, by legitimising men who are 'both the creatures and creators of their beliefs'.[19] His transaction is not unrelated to that of Conrad, except that Conrad sees human wickedness prevailing, where Said provisionally trusts to conscience and character. For Said, Conrad was a modern father figure, with whom he was on familiar terms; Said was closer to him in time and imagination than Vico, who was a distant father to be addressed more formally. The conditions were not right for Sartre to be the object of the same kind of projection. Aside from Sartre's positions on Israel, which greatly disappointed Said, there was no gulf between Jean-Paul and Sartre in the way that there was between Teodor Jozef Konrad Korzeniowski and his pseudonym Joseph Conrad, between Theodor and Adorno or Edward and Said. And exile is key. With a shared experience of being young and lonely in a strange land – Conrad aged sixteen in France, Said aged fifteen in the United States – each inwardly took up the same challenge, which was to reconcile pride with self-deprecation, pessimism with will, the temptation to cheat with an obsession with truth, and the conquest of freedom with simultaneous gratitude. In 1917 Conrad wrote, 'I am no slave to prejudice and formulas, and I never shall be. My attitude to subjects and expressions, the angles of vision, my methods of composition will, within limits, be always changing – not because I am unstable or unprincipled but because I am free.'[20]

Through his agreement and disagreement with Conrad, Edward found his double. He found Said and, in Said, found the strength to contradict Edward. His freedom took shape and, on the last page of his autobiography, asserted itself in terms that proved very similar to Conrad's:

> I occasionally experience myself as a cluster of flowing currents. I prefer this to the idea of a solid self, the identity to which so many attach so much significance. These currents, like the themes of one's life, flow along during the waking hours, and at their best, they require no reconciling, no harmonizing. They are 'off' and may be *out of place*, but at least they are always in motion, in time, in place, in the form of all kinds of strange combinations moving about, not necessarily forward, sometimes against each other, contrapuntally yet without one central theme. A form of freedom, I'd like to think even if I am far from being totally convinced that it is.[21]

In his thesis on Conrad, he anticipated the ideas he later developed in *Beginnings*, and which remained central to all his works: 'The retrospective mode of so many of Conrad's shorter works can be understood as the effort to interpret what, at the time of occurrence, would not permit reflection.'[22]

This is also my approach in writing about Said.

X

The World, the Text and the Critic is the most concise, best written and densest of Said's books. It notably includes a chapter on Foucault and Derrida that sheds some useful light on the work of each, and on Said's own. Here again, Said positions himself by positioning the other. Again, the French method – we could say *French intelligence* – occupies a central place; the use of comparison boosts his critical energy and enables him to indicate nuances and differences. By both training and nature, he was far closer to Foucault, who blazed the trail with his challenge to the established authority of knowledge and norms. Derrida stimulated and irritated him. Catered to his penchant for sophistication, and frustrated his need for reality. Whereas Foucault temporarily brought him both in equal measure. Said borrowed from Foucault's 'toolkit'[1] of concepts to write *Orientalism* and *Culture and Imperialism* and shake the foundations of imperialist knowledge beyond structuralism. The entire question of genealogy, its impurity and disparate, ungraspable nature, fuelled Edward's thinking on discontinuity, which started with *Beginnings*. In that book he describes *Madness and Civilization* as a 'masterful' work. This is not a neutral compliment, Said was rarely unconditional. Above and beyond admiration, he is signalling a reference that would prove crucial over the next two decades, although Said came to distance himself somewhat from Foucault. Indeed, he did so even towards the end of *Beginnings*, in relation to Foucault's vision of man – let us say human beings. Neither object nor entirely subject, in Foucault's work human beings are stripped of the power to consciously resist the flow of contradictory, approximate discourses that they can use to talk about themselves. They are in constant danger of dissolution. They are inherently inadequate, their autonomy limited by the autonomy of knowledge. In a word, they carry their failure within them. Foucault said,

> What I wanted to do – and perhaps it was this that provoked such protest – was to show that the same phenomenon could be seen in the history of human knowledge: the history of human knowledge did not remain in human hands. It is not man himself who consciously created the history of his knowledge, but the history of human knowledge and science itself obeys determining conditions that are beyond us. In this sense, man has nothing left – not language, not consciousness, not even his knowledge.[2]

This vision was later described by Said as 'a system based on stoicism rather than a system that gives rise to intransigence and resistance'.[3] It seems to me that Said was far more prepared to accept, and even endorse, such an admission of powerlessness in the novel, than in critical thought. In reality, there is a strong kinship of pessimism linking Foucault and Conrad's versions of man. This kinship was noted by Said himself in an extract from the end of *Heart of Darkness*. This is the point where Kurtz, who has every gift, starting with that of speech, moves out of the light and into darkness, emptying himself of all the meaning that his words had brilliantly conveyed. Foucault wrote: 'The path from man to true man goes by way of the madman.'[4] But, for all his celebrated scholarship on the treatment of 'madmen' by the authorities down the centuries, did Foucault know madness? I wonder if his view of insanity was perhaps, like Said's, too brilliant, too controlled, to see it from the inside. Of the three contemporary thinkers – Said, Foucault and Deleuze – it is undoubtedly the latter who, by linking thought and disorientation, acquired the means to look at madness closely; in other words, with the greatest possible physical intuition. Like Nietzsche and Dostoevsky. It is no coincidence that the dispute between Foucault and Derrida came to a head around their divergent interpretations of Descartes' view of madness. In Foucault's eyes, Descartes denied the overlap between reason and madness: 'Descartes . . . has now acquired that certainty, and he grasps it firmly: madness, quite simply, is no longer his concern. It would be an eccentricity for him to suppose that he were eccentric; as a way of thinking, madness implies itself, and thus excludes itself from his project. The perils of madness have been quashed by the exercise of Reason.'[5] To which Derrida makes the following objection in *Writing and Difference*:

> The reference to dreams is therefore not put off to one side – quite the contrary – in relation to a madness potentially respected or even excluded by Descartes. It constitutes, in the methodical order which here is ours, the hyperbolical exasperation of the hypothesis of madness . . . *From this point of view* the sleeper, or the dreamer, is madder than the madman.[6]

Rereading both of them, I have the feeling that they are arguing over madness, or the right to think about it, like two children arguing over their mother. They don't like the way that madness knows something they don't. What could be more normal, more human, than to identify with the madman? But what is that part of the self that needs madness to *cover* reason, to legitimate it? And, at the same time, in thinking to give madness the chance to speak, silences it? Is it the guilt of not being mad, the megalomania of wanting to be everything at once, a waking sleeper, a thinker and dreamer, and so on? Or is it another of our neuroses, the kind that wants to enjoy madness by giving pleasure to reason? I peer into this fiercely intellectual debate between two thinkers who, each in their own way, pushed the use of reason to its limits, to try to identify the position adopted by Said, with regard to them and thence to madness itself. It quickly becomes apparent, however cautious he may be in relation to Derrida, that he is resolutely on Foucault's side. His key motive being the fact that Foucault links the history of madness to institutions and authorities, whereas Derrida has it emerge from history's factory as follows:

> This crisis in which reason is madder than madness – for reason is nonmeaning and oblivion – and in which madness is more rational than reason, for it is closer to the wellspring of sense, however silent or murmuring – this crisis has always begun and is interminable. It suffices to say that, if it is classic, it is not so in the sense of the *classical age* but in the sense of eternal and essential classicism, and is as historical in an unexpected sense.[7]

Here we encounter the distinction between origin and beginnings on which, as we have seen, Edward's entire oeuvre is based. In giving the *'unthought'* a passive sense in Derrida and an active sense for Foucault,[8] Said is not merely providing an analysis, but making a choice. He comes down on a particular side. He maintains the balancing point on which all his thought relies: the distinction between beginning and origin and, from there, the choice of the former, called active, rather than the passive time of origins. Close reading of his essay on Foucault and Derrida reveals how, through their debate, Said negotiated his own relationship to time, being and madness. After describing Derrida's approach – a dangerous task to say the least – Edward returns to the criteria that underpin his political thinking. And these criteria undeniably require Foucault's selective method rather than Derrida's shifting sands. 'If everything in a text is always open equally to suspicion and to affirmation, then the differences between one class interest and another, between oppressor and oppressed, one discourse and another, one ideology and another, are virtual in – but never crucial to making decisions.'[9] Said rejected the sense of equivalence he found in Derrida. He needed the support of authority to establish what he was saying. He found it in Foucault, lost it in Derrida. In the final analysis, he leaves the two men to their quarrel and, having taken on their shared dispute with the dominant culture, returns to his own path at the point where literature emerges from its rut of isolation and re-joins its political and historical context. What I am fairly sure of, finally, is that Edward systematically kept madness at a distance, and Foucault, paradoxically, helped him to protect himself. Foucault gave Said a framework in which the madman could be understood, not so much from his own point of view, but through the fear, ignorance and stupidity of those who were not mad. Both writers attacked jailers – the jailers of the mad in Foucault's case, the jailers of the colonised and oppressed in Said's. Although differently – very differently – and whatever they may have said or done, Foucault, Deleuze, Derrida and Said were all overwhelmed by madness, and with good cause. By definition, madness has the power to derail all reason. In practice, Said was the least *tempted* by the subject. Not only was madness unknown to him, he avoided it. In this regard, Frantz Fanon showed unusual boldness and wisdom. As his lucidity in relation to psychological distress did not conflict with his combative power, he continued to occupy an unproblematic place in Said's work. 'Fanon is at once able to diagnose the nature of oppression and to work on the means to end it,' wrote Sonia Dayan-Herzbrun, who, like Pierre Bourdieu, helped break down Edward's solitude among academics in France.[10] 'Foucault's trajectory followed a course diametrically opposed to that of Fanon,' she notes.[11] Despite Foucault's early centres of interest (asylums, prison), he soon became convinced that resistance was largely impossible. 'A kind of quietism emerges in different places in Foucault's career: the feeling that everything is determined. This quietism was accompanied by what Said saw as posing when he met him for the first time in 1978.'[12] Posing? I wouldn't know. It is true that Edward was 'pissed off' by the self-importance he encountered from a number of French intellectuals. Annoyed and disappointed, for French culture was a major part of his own. Nevertheless, Foucault was very important in structuring Said's thought, all things considered, and he could not dismiss this influence or sum it up in a few words. Shortly before his death, he was still observing that Foucault 'was a great philosopher of a kind that no longer exists'.[13]

To conclude, the general movement of Said's thought is characterised by a perpetual back-and-forth between Vico and Foucault. This connection covers the terrain on which he could both deconstruct and consolidate ideas, allowing himself to absorb the impure genealogy observed by the author of *Discipline and Punish*, while simultaneously preserving the rights of history as set out by the author of *The New Science*. These two early theoretical companions were with him to the end, or almost. In *The New Science* Vico describes a kind of jungle lit up by the birth of languages and gods. Here, too, he left a lasting impression on Said, and reassured him. Not only did Vico place God at a distance, he grounded him in mythology. *The New Science* has a strong kinship with the work of the German philologist Auerbach, whose influence on Said never waned. This kinship goes deeper than the unparalleled erudition displayed by both authors and their amazing capacity to explore languages. Auerbach, author of *Mimesis: The Representation of Reality in Western Literature*, translated Vico into German. He is also part of the tradition that fascinated Said, in which encyclopaedic knowledge is freely illuminated through eccentric choices of authors, works and details. It is no coincidence that, unlike his friend Barenboim, Edward chose Vico over Spinoza. The latter puts God in nature, whereas, for Vico, God is the author of nature, but then quits the earthly stage for that of heaven. Being the first to create, he gives men the power that Edward always claimed, to be the authors of the history that begins with them. This division of labour was bound to suit Said: through it his metaphysical unease was managed and absorbed into the physical dimension – throughout his life, Edward worked on the 'discipline of the body' advocated by the author of *The New Science*. Said's penchant for Vico's thought again confirms the autobiographical nature of his literary choices. Having given twin interpretations of Vico's thought, he retraces his steps and sums them up as follows:

> I seem to have reversed my first point about Vico's atavistic method. From seeing his work as an attempt to force theory back into gross physical beginnings, I now have him using theory instead to manufacture a whole private vision of things . . . In the first case with which I began this essay, theory or system – and I shall use the two words to mean an abstract 'seeing' or explanation from above of a mass of experiences – are forced to encounter the body, which they have ignored. Thus the academy is sent back to the huts and forests for its instruction: atavism. In the second case, a theory or system in the hands of an imperious intellect like Vico's encounters a petrified landscape which it proceeds to move by filling the space with activity and objects: invention.[14]

Atavism and intention. This duality – habit redeemed by creation, contradiction undone by a unifying impulse – is also Said's. He goes on: 'My impression is that Vico liked both ways of dealing with history and used them both without being able to forge a made-up *via media*, a concession to logical argument. He seems quite at ease with contradiction, which is not to say, however, that he was careless of making meaning: quite the contrary.'[15] This last sentence could, word for word, be a portrait of Said. As the true narration – *vera narratio* – merges with the word fable,[16] Vico simultaneously offers Said a fable of knowledge and a tool for verification through facts and chronology. Right down to the way that he moved, walked and dressed, Edward showed a mix of atavism and invention. He carried his ancestors' world on his shoulders; his step was half winged, half leaden, and he would suddenly throw off the burden by countering it with a pair of cufflinks, with an elegance somewhere between the aristo-crat and the dandy. Vico secretly guaranteed him 'the eternal order of God' – on which he, Said, turned his back – and left his eccentricity all the space necessary for his equally 'imperious' intellect. If Vico as mentor exerted an ancestor's authority on the story of Said's thought, Foucault's authority was neither entirely that of a father nor quite that of a brother. He was a kind of non-secret companion, a brilliant double forerunner, whom Said was still citing in his last works, but more obliquely.

> And if pointing out these sources – denouncing and speaking out – is to be a part of the struggle, it is not because they were previously unknown. Rather, it is because to speak on this subject, to force the institutionalised networks of information to listen, to produce names, to point the finger of accusation, to find targets, is the first step in the reversal of power . . . The discourse of struggle is not opposed to the unconscious, but to the secretive.[17]

These words of Foucault's, cited by Said,[18] are a perfect summation of the former's influence on the latter's undertaking. Particularly since Said was exploring the domain of imperialism and colonialism, which Foucault had left more or less untouched. The method was useful and the terrain open. By linking Foucault's thought to that of Vico, Said acquired the means to launch a broad process of deconstruction, without depriving himself of a degree of pragmatism – a return to solid ground. Hence his relatively classic eccentricity, or his eccentric classicism, whichever.

XI

Whether battling for Palestine or writing about the western or Arabic novel, the philosophies of Foucault, Vico, Adorno and Auerbach, the different versions of orientalism and imperialism, or the domination of one culture over another, Said was always endlessly, tirelessly dealing with the relationship to time or to the starting point, be it solid or fragile, which the present can use to negotiate its survival and simultaneously create a future. How did Dickens, Stendhal and Tolstoy integrate the past into their novels? Where did they get it? From which authors or furrows ploughed by others before them? All of Edward Said's work can be understood in these terms; it is this aspect that, within its simultaneously inventive and repetitive movement, ensures its non-linear coherence and continuity.

So, *Beginnings* considers the connection between the western genre of the novel and the late appearance of fiction in Arabic, which is 'almost entirely of this century'[1] – the twentieth. How should we understand this time lag, which is also apparent in autobiography – a very rare genre in the Arabic literary tradition? To what can it be attributed? In Chapter 3, Said advances a theory largely ignored in analyses of his writings, and which he himself later set aside, without formally bringing it into question. It concerns the relationship between fiction and the Quran. Said says:

> It is significant that the desire to create an alternative world, to modify or augment the real world through the act of writing

(which is one motive underlying the novelistic tradition in the West) is inimical to the Islamic world-view. The Prophet is he who has *completed* a world-view; thus the word *heresy* in Arabic is synonymous with the verb 'to innovate' or 'to begin'. Islam views the world as a plenum, capable of neither diminishment nor amplification. Consequently stories like those in *The Arabian Nights* are ornamental, variations on the world, not completions of it.[2]

Taking as an example one of the few autobiographical narratives of the early twentieth century – by the Egyptian writer Taha Hussein, who was familiar with both Arabic and western culture – Said highlights the connection between the Quran and the imagination, albeit indirectly, observing that Hussein's narrative style shows 'no resemblance to Quranic Arabic.'

For almost every childhood occurrence narrated by Hussein is in some way connected with the Quran – not as a body of doctrine, but as a presence or fact of everyday life . . . One's impression is that life is mediated by the Quran, informed by it; a gesture or an episode or a feeling in the boy's life is inevitably reduced (always in an interesting way) back to a relationship to the Quran. In other words, no action can depart from the Quran; rather each action confirms the already completed presence of the Quran and, consequently, human existence.[3]

The Arabic word for heresy, which Said refers to at the start of the chapter, is *bid'ah*, originally meaning renewal or invention, and which, when associated with religion – *bid'ah diniyyah* or innovation contradicting the word of God – has the sense of heresy, diversion or deviation. Here, Said opens up a fascinating discussion, with endless ramifications, around the interpretation, instability and mutation of meanings in Arabic and the shifting semantic sands on which visions of Islam are built and destroyed. In this way, he found himself dealing, at an early stage, with a question of method concerning Islam. The idea he advances in *Beginnings*, relating to the Quran's influence on the novel, produced a difficulty that he undoubtedly felt unable to pursue: that of being overwhelmed by the consequences of his discovery, which would have required him to make a detailed study of the Quran. This would have taken him away from his usual mode of work and combat, deep into the religious sphere, which he had only ever viewed at a distance, from a socio-political and cultural perspective. It would also have required him to cede too much ground to religion, implying – as so many commentators are currently tempted to do – that notions in Islamic art and thought have the Quran as their only reference. Ultimately, the great question raised by his hypothesis – and which is more pertinent today than ever – is that of how Muslim religion and culture can be approached from a point of view that is neither offensive nor defensive. How can we deal with the Quranic text and the destiny of two billion people called Muslims without dividing them or, crucially, regarding them as all the same? Without losing sight of the essential point that 'a thousand-year-old religion invents or reinvents itself in every period. Believers unknowingly reconstruct and reconfigure its imaginary and dogmatic landscape according to what they are'.[4] How can a way of representing the world that was set in the seventh, eighth and ninth centuries, in the light of shifting interpretations and in a deeply tribal context, and its multiple versions as they have been modified by history, economics, society and geography, be combined in a – necessarily heterogeneous and contrasting – synthesis? There are certainly dominant, lasting values based on a particular system of representation sustained by texts, transmission, religion and practice. This is true of the three monotheistic religions and religions in general. However, there remains a gap that can never be filled, between a vision of God and the world written 'once and for all', and its evolution over centuries that – negatively and/or positively – maintains or erodes that 'once and for all'. The process is comparable to that which Proust shows us, with the unfillable gap between the past as it was and its retrospective depiction by memory. Every time we try to halt time, to set it in stone, it bounds away in another direction. Words are powerless. Dangerously empty. If they are full of life in *In Search of Lost Time*, it is because they move around in the way that light moves its shadows over time. Islam, locked as it is today inside its five letters, cut off from its time, is a word that has been stifled. Those who seek it, here and there, to attack or defend it, seem to be preventing it from living. More precisely, from breathing, with all that the word 'breathe' evokes of pure air and pollution. And approximation. Not to mention the most important thing – the impossible, yet crucial, identification and distinction of those elements that relate directly to religion from those that, from a religious starting point, are manifestations of custom, transformations, consequences, more or less stated levels of faith or unbelief – in other words, culture in the broad sense. The same is true of the words associated with Islam. How many of us know the etymological meaning of the word *sharî'a*, which I learned on reading Jacqueline Chabbi?

> [*Sharî'a* is] linked to a characteristic of the terrain, access to water in arid Arabia. The image created refers to a reality that is very strong in its context. The *sharî'a* (a feminine word) is a very particular kind of watering place. It is where water rises to the surface . . . In an ideal *sharî'a*, dromedaries can drink directly, without their drivers needing to draw the water up.[5]

It would be an understatement to say that the word has degenerated from its initial meaning to the use made of it by the Wahhabis and doctors of Islamic law. Created to refer to the watering hole that quenched the camel's thirst, today the word serves to legitimate suppression and censorship. Its decay is a symptom of official religious and Arabic discourse at the present time. It is entirely possible that Said's arguments, legitimately used to combat anti-Muslim racism, suffered in part from this deadening of words. Let us say that, in his writing, the Islam distorted by the

American media and experts only incidentally meets the other Islam that has been hijacked by fundamentalism. The sick Islam, in which progress has broken down, contaminating orphaned minds, day after day. In practice, Edward had an avoidance strategy when it came to religion. As we have seen, Giambattista Vico's philosophy of history occupies a huge place in Said's writing and puts Said's Catholic side on hold, although it is central. The 'divine providence' that is omnipresent for the author of *The New Science* is shelved, erased, in the essay entitled 'Vico on the Discipline of Bodies and Texts'.[6] The only God mentioned in these pages is Jupiter, mythological master of the gods. It is true that Vico's own relationship to the Catholic religion was more pragmatic than doctrinal. For him, Catholicism is indispensable to the construction and preservation of the nation, to behavioural consistency. His God is far too useful a convention to be questioned. To return to the imagination in Islam, Said simply moved his cursor, without touching on the relationship between the holy text and human creation, which, from experience, he undoubtedly saw would require him to delve into religion more deeply than he wished. To be precise, he refers briefly to the issue in a chapter of his book *Reflections on Exile* entitled 'Arabic Prose and Fiction after 1948'. It is a reminder in parenthetic form: '(elsewhere I have speculated on one reason for this difference between Arabic-Islamic and European prose fiction: whereas the former literary tradition views reality as plentiful, complete, and divinely directed, the latter sees reality as radically incomplete, authorizing innovation, and problematic)'.[7] We can note that the 'speculation' is prudently left as such and, crucially, that the Quran is replaced here by 'literary tradition'. In passing, we should note that this replacement poses another problem of precision, which no doubt escaped Said's notice. It could suggest that there was no Arabic literary tradition before Islam, which is clearly not the case. Be that as it may, it is fairly certain that, through this lexical swap, Said ensured a continuity that spared him entering the labyrinth of interaction with the 'holy text'. He nevertheless opened up an avenue of exploration that deserves to be followed and freely debated. I use the word 'freely' with intent, since with hindsight it seems clear that, as a whole, the work of Arab intellectuals suffered from a lack of 'freedom' in relation to religion during the second half of the twentieth century. Taboo, trepidation, inhibition, censorship and fear generally prevailed over spontaneity and critical thinking. One cannot help wondering why the writer Adonis, who founded the fascinating journal *Mawâqif* in 1968 and could recite long sections of the Quran by heart, waited fifty years to formulate his indictment of that text. And why an indictment, rather than a critical analysis recognising the right of history to evolve or degenerate? Why so reductive a vision from such a fine mind, so much at home with nuances of thought and language? And why did the situation have to deteriorate on every side – the rise of Islamist fundamentalism and anti-Muslim racism – for Adonis to allow himself to take issue with what he calls the 'violence' of Islam, without considering its context, its history and the vast difference between the letter of a religion and the hundreds of millions of individuals who inherit it at birth? Today we are experiencing the near-psychotic core of this intellectual crisis, which divides thinkers into two equally blinkered halves. On one side are those who dive without a second thought into a simplistic, hasty reading of the text, finding reasons, in this verse or that, to reject wholesale everything that closely or distantly relates to Islam, including Muslims themselves. These people forget, and make their readers forget, that fifty years ago the jihadists' grandparents and great-grandparents, also Muslims, were neither apostles of hate nor candidates for death. And then there are the others, the people who, in their fight against those I have just described, calmly ignore everything in the unreformed Quranic text that seriously undermines basic rights, notably those of women and nonbelievers. These include both blinkered Islamists and people on the left, blinded by the desire to combat a more inflexible secularism and to reconcile the irreconcilable – Islamic dogma and the revolution they have in mind. This latter group includes friends who refuse to accept the fact that Islamism is, in itself, indefensible as a form of political power. We find ourselves in the insane situation where one side suddenly invests colonialism with virtues of every kind, even linking the problems of indigenous peoples to its disappearance. Meanwhile the others see the ravages of colonialism alone as responsible for decline, closing their eyes to the appalling position of women under Islamist regimes and the fascist organisation of a party like Hezbollah, which they choose to view only as an organisation for resistance. As indeed it was, for a while, but at what cost? Today it is a factional army within Lebanon – an army that threatens the army – and, moreover, fully allied to the Assad regime. It would be interesting to know the grounds on which it escapes criticism by French revolutionaries, who, at the same time, sidestep all the issues of religious reform and interpretation that urgently need addressing. Several authors, including the jurist Ali Abdel Raziq in Egypt in the late 1940s, and the philosopher Sadiq Jalal al-Azem in Damascus and Beirut in the late 1960s, courageously launched debates, the former on the need to modernise Quranic teaching and the latter on individual alienation in periods of historic regression. Similarly, the Algerian writer and poet Jamel Eddine Bencheikh – who, with André Miquel, translated the *Thousand and One Nights* into French – strove tirelessly to denounce Islamic obscurantism, without, however, conflating the distinctions within centuries of cultural contrast, during which Islam was used to ends both good and bad. He did not become a hostage to either his original Arabic and Muslim culture or his adopted French culture. When criticising the fanaticism of Algerian Islamists, he also denounced the brutality of the regime and the Algerian army, the lies and corruption of the state. Taking care not to side with one or the other, not to fall into the trap of a false choice between one culture and another, Bencheikh maintained both strands of his thought, criticising the blind spots of East and West in equal measure, while embracing the beauty of both. He was not the only one, likewise Mohammed Arkoun, far from it. I am not qualified to identify the works of the many Arab thinkers who contributed to the advances in critical thinking on Islam in this period. Nor is this my subject. What I can say is that, generally speaking, so-called secular Arab thinkers were intimidated by religion in the last decades of the twentieth century. On the Muslim side this was for more or less conscious, more or less overt reasons of community solidarity, and among progressive Christian Arabs it reflected a similarly unacknowledged concern to maintain balances, in which archaic elements were also present. Religion was untouchable – more or less 'sacred', even for keen readers of Sartre and Nietzsche. The freedom adopted by Bencheikh, who courageously stated in an interview, 'I am an atheist Muslim',[8] was unusual to say the least. The taboo on religion led to a broad suppression of thought, and thereby delayed recognition of the possible danger, in the case of an Arab collapse, of a massive resurgence of Islam as a political force. The collapse, as we know, was not slow in coming. When Edward and I discussed this subject, we were in complete agreement on the absolute necessity of a separation of powers, and he was fiercely critical of the backwardness of Wahhabism, but I was more pessimistic about Islam's potential to invade the political arena. When the Twin Towers collapsed in Manhattan on 11 September 2001, he wrote a remarkable article entitled 'The Clash of Ignorance'. In the first version that he faxed me, he referred to the Islamist terrorists as a 'handful', to which I replied, 'How do you know there's just a handful of them? Who knows the extent of the forest concealed by these trees?' The defenders of the Palestinian cause, heirs to Arab nationalism, were slow to gauge the dangers of Islamism. In Paris in the late 1990s, at weekly meetings with French and Arab friends on the Palestinian issue, I remember casting a chill with my insistence on the danger of Islamism. On the need to incorporate it into the premises of our intellectual struggle. The response – in essence – was, this is not the time, that's not the issue. Around the same time, Said published a new paperback edition of *Covering Islam*, with an introduction in which he talked about the changes that had occurred since the first edition of 1981. In this retrospective text, written sixteen years after the initial publication, Edward fights on two fronts. He rightly maintains the thrust of his book, which is an evidence-based critique of the media's distortion and demonisation of the Muslim world. He also adjusts his aim to take in the complexity of the situation. Notably by painting a very negative picture of Arab countries, including 'such basically Islamic countries as Saudi Arabia, Egypt, Iraq, Sudan, and Algeria'.[9] He strongly condemns dictatorships, authoritarian regimes and the use of torture. Nevertheless, the book focuses primarily on current events in America, avoiding or minimising the situation in relation to Islamic institutions, the gradual desiccation of the imagination in Arab countries and the urgent need for debate on the relationship between temporal and spiritual aspects in the Quran. It goes without saying that Edward's vigilance in denouncing anti-Muslim racism went hand in hand with a loathing of obscurantism on the part of Arab authorities. At the time of the fatwa against Salman Rushdie in 1989, he gave his full support to the author of *The Satanic Verses*, just as he systematically avoided engaging with members of established regimes, rulers, warlords and official representatives of the authorities he challenged. This choice enabled him to write his Reith Lectures[10] on the conditions necessary for intellectual credibility, starting with distance from power. Such a position was uncommon in Arab intellectual circles, where contacts between intellectuals and political rulers were, and still are, widespread to the point of fusion. Where would he stand now? How could he organise his arguments and establish his priorities, when Daesh and Assad have taken evil to the extreme, and the American electorate has brought Donald Trump to power? I will refrain from answering in his absence.

XII

Generally speaking, Edward found criticism hard to deal with. Particularly if it came from minds whose rigour resembled his own. So when, immediately after the publication of *Orientalism*, the Syrian Marxist philosopher Sadiq al-Azem, whose work Edward praised, expressed several reservations about his book, he was hurt. The same was true when Maxime Rodinson, who was very well treated in *Orientalism* – Edward admired his work a great deal – praised his undertaking, but noted important points of disagreement. In essence, according to Rodinson, Said's great merit was to have shaken the self-satisfaction of many orientalists, making them question sources and ideas that might conceal the facts, rather than assume they were natural conclusions, free of prejudice. But, Rodinson observed,

> His militant stand leads him repeatedly to make excessive statements. This problem is accentuated because as a specialist of English and comparative literature, he is inadequately versed in the practical work of the Orientalists. It is too easy to choose, as he does, only English and French Orientalists as a target.[1]

Rodinson's critique is understandable but, in taking issue with Said for not looking at orientalists from non-imperialist countries, he was surely demanding too much. Said couldn't be everywhere at once. He went to the heart of power, deploying exceptional cultural knowledge and making associations that served as examples, without claiming to be exhaustive. He would also undoubtedly have little appreciated Samir Kassir's comments on *Orientalism*, at a conference in Beirut in 2003 (a few weeks after Said's death) to mark the twenty-fifth anniversary of its publication. (Two years later, Samir tragically died aged forty-five, in an attack involving a booby-trapped car.) He notably said, 'For my part, I prefer to remember him as a humanist, rather than imprison him in a single work. Not that *Orientalism* should be ignored or rejected out of hand after twenty-five years, but because, ultimately, the book perhaps posed more questions than it answered.'[2] Kassir was right to emphasise Said's humanism over his sometimes excessive militancy. He was wrong, later in his talk, to link Said's critique of Renan to his marked approval of Rodinson, and wrong too to undervalue the courage and scope of *Orientalism* which, when published in the late 1970s, enabled the next generation – Kassir's – to advance, far better armed than Said's had been, to face the language and devastating wars perpetrated by a particular West against a particular East. As organiser of the launch of the French translation of *Orientalism*, published by Le Seuil in 1980, I can testify to the unbelievable difficulty I had in interesting the French media. Resistance was palpable everywhere, assistance minimal. Intellectuals 'indebted' to Israel had raised a silent, invisible barrier against the book – ruled it inadmissible. This absolved them from the need for a debate in which Edward's eloquence – he spoke excellent French – would have driven them into a corner. I encountered the same difficulty for the next twenty years. I would go from one publisher to the next, with Edward's books under my arm, trying to persuade one of them to publish an author whose work could by then be read in over thirty languages. Nothing doing.[3] It was not until he was near death that these same publishers saw the importance of translating him. Proof or coincidence? By the time the translations were published, he was no longer there to make his arguments. And, I accept, less threatening to his detractors without his formidable capacities as a speaker. *This book perhaps posed more questions than it answered*: in my eyes these overtly critical words are the finest compliment that can be paid to a book like *Orientalism*. If a thinker were required to provide more answers than questions, we would have to draw a line under everything – or almost everything – of importance in the history of thought. The other part of Kassir's critique, made before him by al-Azem, Rodinson and others, is more convincing. It identifies one of the weaknesses of a book that is otherwise very (maybe too) powerful, but could not include all the nuances required by so vast a subject. I can't help feeling a little weary at the idea of entering into the meanders of this debate, a debate that seems to suggest that the thinkers I have just mentioned, and many others, had a fundamentally different vision from Said of the world they wanted to live in. In actuality, they wanted the same world. They fought for the same goals, the same freedom, with the same thirst for justice. And no matter how often I am told that it is naive to try, in the name of a shared humanism, to avoid a debate that continues to rage, I persist, and I state my case: there is something sad, not to say depressing, about strictly intellectual debate. I believe this to be so, particularly as I engaged in debate, every time I had the means or was given the opportunity. And every time, I felt unsatisfied to the point of suffocation. I am talking about a debate that places ideas above people, that ignores the narcissism beneath its brilliance, that readily confuses the need for truth with a need for posterity, and deals with thought as though its fate were temporarily disconnected from death. As though it were healthy people's business. To the extent that we are intelligent, we are all exposed to the dangers of intelligence that is used first and foremost to defend itself. Of course, I don't want to underestimate the importance of 'differences' and 'divergence', which together guarantee the existence of thought itself, its vitality and durability. But I am thinking of the interminable quarrels between individuals whose opinions barely differ, and who undermine the field that their combined efforts could have fertilised, so that, on all sides, they are obliged to deplore its sterility. For my part, I dream of a conference – that invites its participants to discuss the importance of rivalry and jealousy in their writings and their silences. Some hope. Here is another taboo which, had it been broken, would have fostered courage, lightened the atmosphere and brought in a breath of air. Better still, it would have brought back the humour and mockery that our intellectual posturing banishes with dispiriting ease. In this regard, East and West are as bad as each other. On jealousy, Edward would have had a lot to say, about both his own and the jealousy he inspired, then as now. This jealousy was, of course, particularly rife among those working in the same areas as himself. *Orientalism* is a book that lends itself to critiques – I would go so far as to say that critique is crucial to the vitality of its content, to its survival. Its ambition was too great to be fully satisfied, and its subject too complex to permit a definitive thesis. All the same, to ignore its vast scholarship, wealth of arguments, associations and discoveries, its avant-garde nature and the risks taken to write it by an author who was not yet famous, the loud alarm bells it triggered by itself, in a world largely dominated by the heirs to colonial thinking, is to offend, not so much against Said, as against the importance of a book that left academia behind, connecting the luxurious power of knowledge to the rights of people without power and, ultimately, connecting thought to life. According to al-Azem, Said fell into the very trap he denounced – essentialism – by using two distinct notions of East and West. He accused Said of making an abusive, disproportionate link between institutional and academic orientalism. This criticism seems to me partly valid and partly influenced by the systematism it denounces. It is perhaps this interplay of critical perspectives that offers the most faithful, vibrant account of the shifting relationship between East and West, which Edward endlessly described, over and over, as in no way pure or distinct from each other, but mixed and inextricable. It is a shame that we have no documentation of a verbal or written exchange between al-Azem and Said, who had more to learn from each other than to criticise. The academic Abdirahman A. Hussein sums up the content of the debate that continues to this day around this highly controversial book.[4] For my part, I don't want to enumerate the pros and cons of the arguments, paraphrasing this or that author or engaging in a discussion which is, in itself, the subject of a book. I am more interested here in what motivated and activated Edward Said's thought than in the conclusions it reached – if it can be said to have led to any definitive conclusions. For me, its finest aspects are its movement and repetitions, and its power of resistance. By 'power of resistance', I also mean Said's quixotic struggle with his past, and with his double. This duel was where his admiring, conflicted relationship with most of the authors that mobilised his energies was played out. Among those authors were Camus and Orwell.

XIII

Why did Camus and Orwell not attract criticism from Said until the second phase of his work? Camus is never mentioned in *Orientalism* and Orwell only once, in a positive light. It was only fifteen years later that they both came under sustained fire in *Culture and Imperialism*. Said writes:

> Like Orwell, Camus became a well-known writer around issues highlighted in the 1930s and 1940s: fascism, the Spanish Civil War, resistance to the fascist onslaught, issues of poverty and social injustice treated from within the discourse of socialism, the relationship between writers and politics, the role of the intellectual. Both were famous for the clarity and plainness of their style.[1]

The association of Orwell and Camus in Said's mind is no coincidence. Both men pleased and displeased him, for very similar reasons: they were elegant, outside any establishment, aware of social injustice and ahead of their socialist contemporaries in their disillusionment. They were original. Rightly or wrongly, they enjoyed a consensual reputation on both the right and left as humanists above the fray. Given their life histories, both had to adopt positions in relation to colonialism and imperialism. In Said's eyes, their fight on this front ends more or less where their discomfort begins. In *Out of Place*, he does not question the value of their writings, but sees their choices as reflecting a set of convenient accommodations that he, the radical, rejects at all costs. He is, without explicitly saying so, making a comparison. His knowledge and experience of the worlds of both East and West, combined with his determination to defend the oppressed, constantly required him to break ranks. In his political arguments, he chose one aspect of himself over another. In other words, he disregarded his mother. Camus, in relation to his own mother, famously said: 'At this moment people are throwing bombs into the trams of Algiers. My mother could be on one of those trams. If that's justice, I prefer my mother.' I would not have included these words, which have often been cited abusively and distorted, had I not just read Orwell cited by Simon Leys: 'If someone drops a bomb on your mother, go and drop two bombs on his mother.'[2] These two quotations tell us a great deal about the kinship between Orwell and Camus who, unlike Said and Sartre, shared a very strong feeling for nature – plants and animals for Orwell, the quality of light for Camus. Of the three, it was doubtless Edward who was the most viscerally attached to his mother, to whom he wrote daily – or almost (he used carbon paper and kept a copy). He undoubtedly believed that it would never have occurred to him to use his mother as a reference in an argument about political choices. We know, through the portrait of her in his autobiography, that to disregard this omnipresent figure in favour of coherent political thought was no small affair. In other words, above and beyond argument, there was rivalry in the air. For Said, Camus and Orwell were fraternal rather than paternal figures. The passages he writes on them, together and separately, are very uneven in tone and style. The analysis he offers in *Culture and Imperialism* is solid, extensive and backed up with quotations. The text entitled *Tourism among the Dogs: On George Orwell* is written in a loose, chaotic style that is hard to read.[3]

Orwell's sustained political writing career coincides not with his down-and-out years, nor with his brief interest in the concrete experience of imperialism (*Burmese Days*), but with his readmission to and subsequent residence inside bourgeois life. Politics was something he observed, albeit as an honest partisan, from the comforts of bookselling, marriage, friendship with other writers (not by any means with the radicals used as material for *The Road to Wigan Pier* and *Homage to Catalonia* and then dropped), dealing with publishers and literary agents.[4]

A few lines further, Said goes in harder: 'Orwell needed to surround himself with a familiar atmosphere that eliminated all worries before he could formulate a position.' A little later he plunges the knife in: 'Just as surely, the off-stage presence of home and the possibility of a phone call for money to Eric Blair's Aunt Nellie constitute the narrator's bad faith when he was a *plongeur* in Paris or a tramp in England.' *A phone call for money to Aunt Nellie . . .* This childish pique contrasts with Said's maturity when he writes about Beethoven and Foucault in *The World, the Text and the Critic*. Intended to knock Orwell off his pedestal, this little phrase signifies: some people work hard for their living, rigour and independence, at the price of great solitude, while others pass themselves off as heroes, tried and tested by poverty, when in fact they have support networks and the resources of those with a private income. Not to mention that Orwell and Said shared a key father figure, Jonathan Swift, for whom both felt immense admiration – though, in passing, Edward observed that Swift was 'in many ways a limited and humanly unattractive figure'.[5] Shortly before his mother's death, he adapted these words to describe two of his other mentors: Conrad and Vico.[6] Let us say that, where Swift was concerned, Edward initially followed Orwell: 'Orwell does not try to prove that by virtue of style or technique the author is really progressive. Quite the contrary, Orwell insists that "in a political and moral sense" he is against Swift even though "curiously enough he is one of the writers I admire with the least reserve".'[7] These lines suggest that Said aligns with Orwell. But, in those that follow, he changes tone and defends his own Swift against Orwell's. 'To say of Swift that he "did not like democracy" is to say something of great irrelevance to the context of the time, since not even Swift's enemies of the "progressive party", to which Orwell alludes quickly in passing, could be described as believers in democracy.' Said is already high-lighting Orwell's apolitical aspect, which would later cause him to write that 'far from having earned the right to denounce social-ism *from within* Orwell had no knowledge either of Marx or of the massive Marxist and socialist traditions; moreover he consist-ently referred to English radicals as "the pansy Left", and seemed totally uninterested in any social or economic analysis that was neither journalistic (like his) nor anti-Marxist.'[8] He goes on to note,

> Orwell seems unable to realize that one can be steadfastly opposed to tyranny, as Swift was all his life, and not have a well-developed position on 'representative institutions' . . . Swift is very much a part of his time: there is no point therefore in expecting him to think and act like a prototype of George Orwell since the cultural options, the social possibilities, the political activities offered Swift in his time were more likely to produce a Swift than an Orwell.[9]

Paradoxically, Said's argument in favour of Swift is not very different from that of Simon Leys defending Orwell against those who see him as a fake socialist, saying, 'It is true that on some of the most burning issues of our time – totalitarianism, paci-fism – Orwell's views are indeed very close to those of the neo-conservatives. But so what? That is not enough to turn him into a member of the new right.'[10] Behind these questions that continue to generate so much comment – who's a real socialist, who's a fake, who's on the right, who's on the left – there is another that intellectuals carefully avoid raising, on pain of seeming naive. I pose it openly, and for myself alone. Is being a socialist, being progressive, a matter of theoretical positions, behaviour or, to use one of Orwell's favourite words, 'decency'? I tend to think that

Orwell and Said are far closer in this regard than Said chose to admit, in the sense that both were repelled by the gap between rich and poor and the relations between dominant and dominated. Orwell's approach was more painterly than analytical, Said more analytical than activist. They both came from backgrounds that could hardly be described as poor. They shared the same sense of guilt and duty. The same loathing for replete, self-satisfied minds. The following description of Orwell by Leys applies also to the Said of *Out of Place*:

> The feelings of abandonment, guilt and failure that had weighed him down as a child never really left him throughout the rest of his life. They inspired in him a sense of duty and obsession with self-punishment on the one hand and, on the other, a visceral anarchism, instinctive rebellion against all established authority, leading him in all circumstances to spontaneously espouse the cause of the poor, the weak and the oppressed.[11]

All this, which, at the very least, preserved them from indifference and cowardice, did not preserve either from a degree of insensitivity to the sufferings of their friends and family. As Leys elegantly puts it, 'ultimately life managed neither to conquer nor to break him – but the same cannot be said of the woman who "took the risk of loving him", his first wife, an admirable person who literally died of cancer before his eyes without his noticing, preoccupied as he was by concern for the sufferings of humankind.'[12] In copying out these words I am reminded of something that makes me smile: Edward and I were sitting in a hotel foyer talking about the problems caused by his chemotherapy. I alluded to one of these, which I knew from my own experience. 'Ah yes, by the way, you've had cancer too!' said Edward, with barely a flicker of embarrassment at having forgotten. In Orwell's case, Leys concludes, a little hastily for me, 'that an innocent of his calibre is clearly much more dangerous than a cynic'. I have a little trouble with this notion of innocence. I don't believe it applied to Orwell or Said. Neither was either innocent or cynical. While undoubtedly very different in temperament, both were driven by a need to reach truths that were hard to say and hear and that did not necessarily benefit their past. They were ready to pay the price. Both had a mission to repair a divide: between Blair and Orwell and between Edward and Said. Said's severity towards Orwell essentially relates to the 'comfort' Orwell preserved during his period of stated discomfort. What kind of comfort? 'The risks of politics were handled from the perspective of someone who very definitely felt, and really was, at home *somewhere*.'[13] Here we have reached the dividing line drawn by Said between the man who feels at home and those who, like Genet, Auerbach and even Conrad to a degree, are like him: *out of place*. He often cited Adorno's words 'It is part of morality not to be at home in one's home', a shortcut that serves as a guide in reading all of Said's work. It explains his comparative indulgence towards the stateless Cioran, whose vision of history was entirely contrary to his own. It may also shed light on one of the reasons why he paid more attention to Derrida than to Sartre, although in terms of method and ideas he was far closer to Sartre.[14] In tandem with its complement – a lack of property – the phrase casts light into every corner. It is no coincidence that, in his portrait of Swift, Said twice notes, with empathy, that Swift did not own any property, and never amassed anything resembling a fortune.[15] I don't own a car or a house, Said told Charles Glass, unasked, in his last interview. This wasn't the first time that Said brought the question of material comfort and property into his thinking. It is true that he didn't own property, but his work gave him complete material security. When I suggested selling my apartment in Paris, so that we could rent somewhere to live in New York, he replied, 'Yes, but the apartment will be small. Where shall I put my second piano?' I recall him saying this with tenderness now. He was undoubtedly less keen to live with me, and more attached to life with his family, than he cared to confess either to me or to himself. With hindsight, I also think that he wasn't wrong to worry about the consequences of turning our magical, *out of place* relationship into cohabitation. All this said, why did a man who, twenty years earlier, had praised Orwell for denouncing the obliteration of the Oriental in European eyes[16] suddenly view him so harshly? I can only think that, with the passing of the years, he came to find the adulation of Orwell, as a man of privation and sacrifice, exasperating in the extreme. The controversy around Orwell's possible role as an informer, passing a list of names of journalists and intellectuals who were 'sympathisers of the Soviet Union' to a department of the British Foreign Office in 1949, had not yet arisen when Said wrote those words. It did not emerge until 1996, three years after the publication of *Culture and Imperialism*. So Edward knew nothing of these accusations – which have been revised and challenged by many – at the time when he was writing about Orwell. It is true that he had just read the books by Peter Stansky and William Abrahams – *The Unknown Orwell* and *Orwell: The Transformation* – and took from them elements that reflect what he called Orwell's 'unbelievably apolitical awareness'. It is also true that Orwell proclaimed a relationship to socialism based on what he called 'common sense' and 'common decency', rather than ideology. In *Some Thoughts on the Common Toad*, he wrote, 'I think that by retaining one's childhood love of such things as trees, fishes, butterflies and – to return to my first instance – toads, one makes a peaceful and decent future a little more probable.'[17] Let us say that this vision, this language, was unlikely to find an echo in Said. Although the same phrase from another writer might have done so. For my own part, I was always telling him how little I liked dogma, political parties and the ideas of the self-satisfied left, without ever offending him. Edward was very sensitive to things that disturbed the conventional order of ideas. When Simon Leys notes that 'in the normal order of priorities, frivolity and the eternal should come before politics',[18] there is no reason to think that Edward, with his penchant for frivolous conversation and elegant dress, would have disagreed. But he also had a combative seriousness, which permitted poetry, cynicism and humour only at times of his choosing. Disconnected from any power relation or competition. There were too many similarities between the course of his life and Orwell's, and they were separated by too many issues of form, for their divergence not to degenerate, in his mind, into fierce rivalry. Particularly as the general consensus celebrating Orwell showed Said what his own radical positions had cost him, and would continue to cost him after his death. There are biographical similarities between the young Eric Blair and the young Edward Said. To very different degrees, both inherited a family history linked to Empire. And both rebelled against it. As we have seen, Edward's father had served in the American army. That of Blair – the future Orwell – owed his prosperity to the British Empire; indeed, his great-grandfather had been a slave owner in Jamaica. Orwell was born in India in 1903 and, in 1922, through family connections, became a sergeant of the Imperial Police in Burma. He was nineteen, the age of turning points in the lives of both Conrad and Said – the Marseille episode for Conrad, the Swiss episode for Said. The moment at which the choice to repay the debt was made. And gradually, the 'shadow line' between youth and adulthood appeared. Orwell threw in the towel in 1927, turning against the imperialism he had served, in loneliness and boredom at first and later with a sense of disgust. Then came essays and novels reflecting his hostility to imperialism, totalitarianism and social organisation that marginalises the poor. At what point did his experience on the ground, among Yorkshire labourers and the Middlesbrough unemployed, cost him his comfort? Whatever the answer to this question, I can't help thinking that Edward settles it in terms more personal than political. He ignores Orwell's health problems – severe pneumonia at the age of twenty-seven and a bullet in the neck in 1936, when he was involved in the Spanish Civil War – portraying him only as an opportunist of 'comfortable concern'.[19] Why is Said so much more indulgent towards Conrad than towards Orwell? (Both regarded themselves as conservative anarchists, the major nuance being that Orwell

EDWARD SAID: HIS THOUGHT AS A NOVEL

hoped for social progress, whereas Conrad hoped for nothing.) In part, this difference of approach relates to the fact that, in Said's eyes, Conrad is a great novelist, while Orwell, with his simple style, is not, but also – and crucially – to the fact that, unlike Orwell, Conrad was living in a land that was not his own, and his 'concern' relates to an anxiety with which the author of *Out of Place* fully identifies. In practice, Said and Orwell do not have the same relationship to time. Said went back over the past, enabling us to read it differently. Orwell looked into the future, which he enabled us to read in advance. Said doesn't say this. The Newspeak invented in 1949 by the author of *1984* is more than just a premonitory vision; it is a vision with implications that are still being verified. I am not sure that intellectuals, who are still using vocabulary from fifty years ago, are in a position to gauge the degree of devastation suffered by language on a global scale. Perhaps we are also not in a position to imagine its return – the renaissance of language – which can still happen after the destruction of words. 'It's a beautiful thing, the destruction of words', says Syme. 'Of course the great wastage is in the verbs and adjectives, but there are hundreds of nouns that can be got rid of as well. It isn't only the synonyms; there are also the antonyms. After all, what justification is there for a word which is simply the opposite of some other word?'[20] All in all, it seems to me that, in his critique of Orwell, Said was overpowered by a dimension that was not strictly intellectual or political. His sarcastic tone speaks more of a quarrel between brothers than a fundamental disagreement. It is not a reduction of Edward's work to attribute to it an element of emotion. I would say that, in his case, the opposite would be more true; to eliminate the emotional, personal element of his thought is to reduce it, to deprive it of an important aspect of its texture, its colour and even its raison d'être. While all thought undeniably has elements of story, there is more story in his than in that of others.

This is where Camus comes in. And, with him, the issue of thought as a novel, the relationship between experience and ideas.

Imagination and essays. Atavism and rebellion. And the inevitable element of bad faith that, to different degrees, we all carry within us, and which allows us to escape, now and then, from the truth that threatens the foundations of both our memories and our equilibrium. Bad faith in the sense Sartre discussed (in relation to the waiter who plays at being a waiter), which has us playing a role down to the most minute gesture, and at the price of freedom.[21] But also, bad faith as a screen or defence mechanism. As protection against inner storms. These storms come at different times and in different forms, depending on the period, author and work. They are at their most threatening in times of war. They can weaken or strengthen words, but not figures. Without bad faith there would undoubtedly be no poetry, nor even thought. We are living through a historical period in which numbers are much more powerful than words. What has this to do with Camus, you might ask, what has it to do with Said? Before I answer I'd like to say something more. I would like to add that our need for bad faith is almost as vital to our narcissism as the need for God is vital to humanity, as history proves. There might be too much or too little bad faith in this writing and, to remedy the lack or excess, I am relying on the 'calm awareness that I might perhaps be wrong'.

What Said shows us in Camus is his relationship to French colonialism, his denial – or rather the position of superiority from which he views, i.e. does not view, the Arabs. In *Algerian Chronicles* he says, 'Believe me when I tell you that Algeria is where I hurt at this moment, as others feel pain in their lungs.'[22] Said understood this. What he challenged was the erasure of history from Camus' arguments – 1830, or France's military conquest of a land that did not belong to it. To put it crudely, the theft of a country. Once again it is an issue of the 'beginning'. Who does this country belong to? This is a discussion Said had more than once with his friend Barenboim, for whom the beginning of Israel's wrongdoing dated from the occupation of 1967, whereas for Said it necessarily dated back to the foundation of the state of Israel in 1948. Here is what Camus says:

As far as Algeria is concerned, national independence is a formula driven by nothing other than passion. There has never yet been an Algerian nation. The Jews, Turks, Greeks, Italians or Berbers would be as entitled to claim the leadership of this potential nation. As things stand, the Arabs alone do not comprise the whole of Algeria. The size and duration of the French settlement, in particular, are enough to create a problem that cannot be compared to anything else in history. The French of Algeria are also natives, in the strong sense of the word. Moreover, a purely Arab Algeria could not achieve that economic independence without which political independence is nothing but an illusion. However inadequate the French effort has been, it is of such proportions that no other country would today agree to take over the responsibility.[23]

Camus' emotions would not allow him to accept the logic of history – the legitimacy of Algerian independence. And, in so doing, deprived him of any kind of understanding or intimacy in relation to the colonised Algerians. For Said's critique does not only address Camus' colonial vision, but also the contradiction between, on the one hand, his call for an Algeria for all, and, on the other, his French vision of the country. As Said says, this vision is reflected in his novels by a striking absence of Arabs. The Arabs do not exist or, when they do, appear only in the form of a fog of people with tanned skins, swirling around his own people. With the exception of a secondary character in *The Mute* – called Said – they have neither name, face nor individual identity. Camus' only posthumous work, *The First Man*, begun in 1953, is a partial exception to the rule. In an essay entitled 'L'Arabe dans les écrits d'Albert Camus', Oran-based Algerian writer Ahmed Hanifi identifies, without preconceptions, the number of times that Arabs are mentioned in Camus' work, and in what form. He establishes a difference between writings published before the outbreak of the War of Independence in 1954, and those written during or after the war.

The harder Algeria fought for independence, the more Camus had to give at least some acknowledgement of Muslim Algerians in the world of his novels. Hanifi also rightly emphasises the discrepancy between the vision of Camus' fiction and that of his essays. In psychoanalytic language, this discrepancy is more or less the same as that between consciousness and the unconscious. Camus always had to negotiate between the two. Between what he thought and what he felt. There is a constant moral crisis within him, which, for lack of a cynicism he tried to cultivate, he could not resolve. Unlike Sartre, he does not want to grant the rights of sensibility and beauty to reason – in which he only half believes. Just as he does not want to give his sensibility a monopoly over his relationship to the Other. Hence the sometimes painful split between thought and fantasy, argument and feeling, in his vision of Algeria. Hence, also, the literary weakness of *The Rebel* compared to his masterpieces *The Outsider*, *The Fall* and *Summer*. In *The Rebel*, intellectual voluntarism drags the writing away from his kingdom, which is sunlight. In the other three, the unconscious triumphs, in language that is as free as the air between sea and sun. If Conrad accepts his own conclusions more fully and clearly, it is because his scepticism is remorseless. Aware that colonialism is cunning, he sums it up in terms that Camus could not have felt entirely happy with, as shown in this extract from *Heart of Darkness*, cited as a leitmotif in Said's work:

> The conquest of the earth, which mostly means the taking it away from those who have a different complexion or slightly flatter noses than ourselves, is not a pretty thing when you look into it too much. What redeems it is the idea only. An idea at the back of it; not a sentimental pretence but an idea; and an unselfish belief in the idea – something you can set up, and bow down before, and offer a sacrifice to.[24]

For Camus, the idea is not enough. He also wants justice. And when justice challenges the equilibrium of his own people, he still wants it, but without 'looking too closely'. In his novels, French and Spanish Algerians are looked at closely, individually, they have lives, but the Arabs do not. They exist, but they do not live; they are seen from afar, en masse. What Said puts his finger on in his analysis is that Camus himself has an inner struggle – the temptation of comfortably belonging to his *own people* at the expense of the *others*. Through their life choices and social class, his *own people* – his family – were cosmopolitan members of the bourgeoisie, cut off from ordinary people. In a lecture given in November 1998 at Birzeit University, I talked about the way that French travellers in the eighteenth and nineteenth centuries viewed the Arabs. The following extract sheds light on the reasons why some have confidently asserted, or thought, that Palestine was a 'land without people for a people without land'. Evoking the presence of 'our Arabs', Lamartine says, 'Their civilisation consists in murder and pillage.'[25] Chateaubriand is no less eloquent, saying of 'these Arabs who infest the deserts' that, 'while the mouth remains shut there is nothing about them to indicate the savage; but as soon as they begin to speak, you . . . hear a harsh rough language very strongly aspirated.'[26] His judgement of Arab women is equally agreeable: 'One should view them from some distance, settle for an overview and not go into detail.'[27] Pierre Loti is enchanted by Islamic art and readily describes 'the fairy splendour' of the Jerusalem Mosque, but he shows it empty, without a living soul inside, as though shut away in a museum. What he says about the Jews goes beyond the pale. The extracts I read to Palestinian students perfectly illustrated the ideas Edward expounded to them concerning the common roots of orientalism and anti-Semitism. 'Anti-Semitism and anti-Arab racism go hand in hand', he would say. 'The roots of orientalism are the same as those of anti-Semitism.'[28] The points in common between the two racist modes of representation do not, however, rule out some fundamental differences. So, Loti – to mention only him – expresses a twofold Catholic and ethnic racism, which I think has no equivalent:

Penetrating the heart of Jewry, my impression above all is a sick feeling, almost terror. Nowhere had I seen such an exaggeration of those kinds of clothes, rags and rabbit skin's merchants; nowhere such sharp pointed noses, so long and so pale. Each time one of these old backs, bent under fur and velvet, half turns towards me, a new pair of eyes looks sideways at me, underneath glasses, between hanging curls. I feel a little surge of surprise and disgust.[29]

This chapter is not the subject of the present book. However, it gives me an opportunity to recall the failures of school and university education in Arab countries. There is no reason, aside from manipulation and confusion, that the fight against Israeli policy should be described as anti-Semitic, just as it is foolish for this same fight to maintain Arab ignorance of anti-Semitism. Edward repeated this over and over.

To return now to Camus, what was the 'colonial unconscious' that Said talked about? Let us look at *The Outsider*. It uses the word 'Arab', singular or plural, a total of twenty-four times. Not once is the word accompanied by a characteristic that would distinguish one Arab from another. Here, side by side, are the moments where, while they don't have a face, the Arabs do have a verb: 'Near the coffin there was an Arab nurse in a white smock' – 'We came upon our two Arabs' – 'the Arabs were moving slowly, they were now a lot closer to us' – 'the Arabs backed away from us and hid behind the rock' – 'Their muffled whispers, rising from below, created a kind of soft background music' – 'The murmuring of the Arabs continued beneath us' – 'the Arab pulled out his knife and raised it towards me in the sun'. The succession of images evokes the beauty of animal movement, the movement of snakes. In *The Plague*, originally published in 1947, when the threat of open conflict between colonisers and colonised was becoming more definite, Arabs appear three times. Reduced almost to nothing, they are less threatening and much more fully ignored than in *The Outsider*. Yet, in the book, the plague that overcomes the city would have struck Arabs as well as Europeans. Simply from reading this novel, who would imagine for a second that forty per cent of the city's 300,000 inhabitants were Arabs? There are the wild Rieux, Tarrou, Paneloux, Grand, Cottard, Castel, Othon and Rambert, but not one non-European. We learn, in passing, that Rambert has asked 'for information about the condition of the Arabs', and that a tobacconist 'had spoken about a recent arrest that had caused a stir in Algiers. It involved a young company employee who had killed an Arab on a beach'.[30] These two occurrences are not as incidental as they seem. Camus distances non-Europeans from the issues and ordeal that the plague represents. He mentions the Arabs only in the light of his ever-present uneasiness and guilt, relating to his awareness of their economic and social penury (Rambert's enquiry into the living conditions of the Arabs) and the associated threat of upheaval, against which the White Man would be tragically tempted to fight (a company employee kills an Arab on a beach). This man could be Meursault, the title character of *The Outsider*.

As a member of the Communist Party from 1935 to 1937 and author of a report on the *frightful* 'penury of Kabylia' in 1939, Camus was never insensitive to poverty and the inequality of living conditions. He faced and fought against them, directly and empathetically. He knew them from experience. But there was something else about the Arabs that he avoided and could not face directly. And that something is too closely linked to elements that frighten people and unhinge minds today to leave it unexplored. Behind the idea that Camus could not accept, could not imagine – Algerian independence – lay something he found hard to recognise and thus to name: fear. Camus was afraid of the 'Arabs' and he wanted even less to do with this fear than with the Arabs themselves. He ignored it, or treated it with scorn. 'The absurd' was his outlet. Camus was afraid of Arabs in broad daylight. At noon. In the sun. In practice, Arabs meant Muslim Algerians. Drawing up a methodical list of the occurrences of the word Arab in his fiction, we see this fear take shape – like print from a negative – until it resembles anxiety, even panic. It can be compared to the 'contact phobia' described by Canetti at the start of *Crowds and Power*. In 'The Adulterous Woman', a story that Said analysed in detail, it can be felt even more strongly than in *The Outsider*. The Arabs are everywhere and nowhere, omnipresent, phantom-like, disturbing. The story starts with a fine description of a fly:

> A housefly had been circling for the last few minutes in the bus, though the windows were closed. An odd sight here, it had been silently flying back and forth on tired wings. Janine lost track of it, then saw it light on her husband's motionless hand. The weather was cold. The fly shuddered with each gust of sandy wind that scratched against the windows.[31]

A poor, exhausted, shivering fly, threatened by the wind and the closed windows. Some time has to pass in this bus juddering over potholes in the road before 'suddenly the wind was distinctly heard to howl . . . The sand now struck the windows in packets as if hurled by invisible hands. The fly shook a chilled wing, flexed its legs and took flight'. Five lines further on, 'The bus was full of Arabs pretending to sleep, shrouded in their burnooses. Some had folded their legs on the seat and swayed more than the others in the car's motion. Their silence and impassivity began to weigh upon Janine; it seemed to her as if she had been traveling for days with that mute escort.' From the extreme detail of the fly, as irritating as remorse, to the uniform blur of the Arab mass, threatening and disturbing, there is room to accommodate almost all of Camus' disquiet. There is also, consciously or not, the response of Camus the writer to Sartre the philosopher, who, in *Combat*, had declared Camus unfit for the world of ideas. Given that the falling-out between Camus and Sartre became definitive at the time when 'The Adulterous Woman' was published, I can hear Camus saying to Sartre, as he writes about his fly, 'You don't think I can think, let's see if all your flies put together are worth a tiny fraction of mine in literary terms'. In Sartre's play *The Flies*, published in 1943, a year after *The Outsider*, the gods have sent insects to Argos to torment its guilty inhabitants. Sartre has Orestes say: 'A crime that its doer disowns becomes ownerless – no man's crime; that's how you see it, isn't it? More like an accident than a crime.'[32] Read in the light of the future feud between the two men, this phrase rings like the Arab's answer to Meursault's friends from beyond the grave. Said's answer to Camus. And here we are again, at the heart of the debate generated by the author of *Culture and Imperialism*. What is the link between the Camus of *The Plague*, who does not show us a single Arab affected by the disease that devastates the city, and the Camus of *Algerian Chronicles* who, when the plague of famine strikes, uses his pen to plead the Arabs' cause?

> The news that must be shouted from the rooftops is that most Algerians are experiencing a famine. This is the reason for the serious disturbances we have heard about, and this is what needs fixing. The population of Algeria is nine million in round numbers. Of these nine million, eight million are Arabo-Berbers, compared with a million Europeans. Most of the Arab population is scattered throughout the vast country-side in *douars*, which French colonial administrations have combined into mixed villages. The basic diet of the Arabs consists of grains (wheat or barley), consumed in the form of couscous or flatbread. For want of grain, millions of Arabs are suffering from hunger.[33]

As we have just seen, figures are less permeable to inner divisions than words. Eight million Arabs for a million Europeans is no small thing. Camus does not mince his words, but abstraction is still a shield, the eight million are still a mass. The vocabulary of journalism creates a seal, protecting him from his subject. Would Camus have settled for the words 'serious disturbances' had he been referring to tens of thousands of deaths among the French of Algeria? Almost certainly not. What is certain is that he does not flinch from detail, when it comes to defending the basic rights of those he keeps at a distance by calling them 'the Arabs'. He cannot fight his fear of losing Algeria and his fear of the Arabs. He can only seek a third way. He does not, and cannot, have the political courage of the Martiniquan Frantz Fanon, who took up the cause of Algerian independence. Of course, unlike Camus, Fanon was not Algerian. His gut feelings did not blur his vision. And, to the wrong suffered by the 'mute mass' of Algerian Arabs, he gave a name: colonisation.

> The first thing which the native learns is to stay in his place, and not to go beyond certain limits. This is why the dreams of the native are always of muscular prowess; his dreams are of action and of aggression. I dream I am jumping, swimming, running, climbing; I dream that I burst out laughing, that I span a river in one stride, or that I am followed by a flood of motor-cars which never catch up with me. During the period of colonization, the native never stops achieving his freedom from nine in the evening until six in the morning.
> The colonized man will first manifest this aggressiveness which has been deposited in his bones against his own people. This is the period when the niggers beat each other up, and the police and magistrates do not know which way to turn when faced with the astonishing waves of crime in North Africa.[34]

In fighting colonialism, Fanon did not sacrifice lucidity to idealism or angelism. As a psychiatrist, he was familiar with the responses of human nature in the face of oppression. He predicted, described and treated them. He knew all about the time bomb in the silent passivity of those who live under the yoke of domination. Fighting colonialism was his clear priority. His human intelligence did not let him forget that yesterday's victim can become tomorrow's executioner. A year after his death, in July 1962, his understanding was confirmed by the massacre of the Algerian French in Oran. Had he survived to see Algerian independence, there is no reason to think that he would have been welcome in one-party Algeria. This does not alter the overall justice of his fight. Any more than the savage, gratuitous destruction of Dresden in 1945 undermines the political line of the allies. Horrors committed in times of victory are an indictment of human nature. Which should help us to understand the Islamist madness that is now winning minds all over the world. If Said so admired in Fanon what Camus lacked, it was because he, too, knew the hatred that feeds on the humiliation of peoples. It was as a Palestinian aware of the extent of the damage to come. He knew, as did Fanon, but not always Sartre or Camus, that the impunity of Israel, supported by the predominantly Christian West, could ultimately give rise to blind, uncontrollable and boundless revenge. Of Fanon, Said wrote,

> His notion was that unless national consciousness at its moment of success was somehow changed into a social consciousness, the future would hold not liberation but an extension of imperialism. His theory of violence is not meant to answer the appeals of a native chafing under the paternalistic surveillance of a European policeman and, in a sense, preferring the services of a native officer in his place. On the contrary, it first represents colonialism as a totalizing system nourished in the same way – Fanon's implicit analogy is devastating – that human behaviour is informed by unconscious desires.[35]

By aligning himself with Fanon's positions, which destroy those of Camus along the way, and by emphasising the need to transform national struggle into social struggle, Said restates in different terms his concern in relation to Palestine. His battle was less for a nation and more for the recognition of injustice; for a justice ready, once its rights had been recognised, to turn back to the Other. This is one reason why he was so strongly opposed to the Oslo Accords in 1993. Those Accords recognised the PLO as representatives of the Palestinians, instead of recognising 'first and foremost' that an entire people had been stripped of their rights. Moreover, they did not provide for the restitution of land or any halt to colonisation. Though claiming to bring peace, they could ultimately only exacerbate both divisions between Palestinians and the war between the two peoples. Am I moving away from Camus' Algeria by talking about Said's Palestine? I think not. At a time when the world is governed by Trump, Putin, Erdogan, Netanyahu, Modi and a China as little socialist as it is possible to be, it is extremely tempting to cut oneself off from history, declare the end of the past and put one's faith in a future that is, by definition, beginning badly. With, in addition, the threat of competition between artificial and human intelligence, which could turn into a mortal struggle. Or worse still, the mirroring of the one intelligence by the other – their fusion. To the destruction of liberty. 'The imperialist regime of truth' denounced by Said is not behind us. Far from it. But it is becoming harder and harder to describe, given the degree to which one lie is infiltrated by another that supposedly contradicts it. In a way, like Camus, Said belonged to that category of humanists whose works and lives unfolded publicly in a world with more or less clear dividing lines, notably between space and time. That world is disappearing. Today's humanists are far more isolated. Disparate. Globalisation aside, they face the challenge of robotisation, which very few of them have the capacity to evaluate and predict. In short, amateur intellectuals, whom Said so preferred to 'the experts', no longer have the capabilities and visibility they once did. So much so that, with hindsight, Said's stated disagreements with Camus lose some of their vigour, and acquire a new form of currency. Together, Said and Camus represent the two sides of a debate that the media do not allow us to have. A space where contradictory arguments provide an opportunity to think, rather than a reason to turn our backs on all that is not us. The opposite of the oppressive head-to-heads between the champions of for and against, which we are constantly fed. Edward's position, which I fully share in political terms, gives us much to think about right now. I want to talk about the inner conflict between fear and reason, which, with the rise of Islamism, presents people with false choices. With the temptation – also felt by Camus – to think of Muslims as a threatening mass. This is a vision that accepts the most dangerous of methods, confusing individuals with verses from the Quran, adopting the peculiarities of the fundamentalism it denounces by confusing the person with the mass, the seventh century with the twenty-first. And there is that other temptation, also blind, that leads some militant anti-imperialists to dismiss those who are frightened by Islam.[36] The highly intellectual temptation to choose intelligence over understanding, to ignore fear in the name of the idea – or in the name of the ideal, which comes to more or less the same thing. To forget, as Fanon said, that an oppressed mind contains the seed of a future oppressor.

XIV

This morning a man killed twenty-two people and wounded more than fifty, including many children, at the end of a pop concert in Manchester. A little over two years ago, in 2015, there was carnage in Paris at the offices of *Charlie Hebdo*, and then in a kosher supermarket, and then, ten months later, at a rock concert by the group Eagles of Death Metal in Bataclan. In the years that preceded and followed, dozens of attacks took place in India, China, Indonesia, Nigeria, Egypt, Iraq, Syria, Lebanon, Yemen, Pakistan, Turkey, Tunisia, Belgium, Sweden and the United States. As well as the symbolic targets that ISIS selects for massacres – churches, Shia mosques, Jewish places of meeting and worship, venues for rock and pop concerts – they also strike airports, hotels and metros. Overall, the most numerous victims are Muslims, and the populations most threatened in existential terms are Christians, Yazidis and other minority faith groups in the Middle East. Edward's work certainly gives us many tools for thinking about these issues. But it did not anticipate the scale of the disaster. Notably, it did not register the threat hanging over Arab Christians. In struggling with all his might against the fear and scorn expressed by western racists for Arabs and Muslims, his vision minimised the danger represented by the revenge of religion. It was certainly hard to do otherwise. Blows were raining down from all sides. He gave priority to the fiercest. I remember one day I was with him in New York, in a television studio of the Qatari station Al Jazeera.

He was giving an interview, which I was watching onscreen in the room next door. Everything had started normally, when I suddenly saw the trap set by the journalist: by whipping up Said's criticism of the Palestinian Authority, he made Said say something he didn't say, twisting Said's words to give a kind of blank cheque to the Islamists. By chance, the programme was in two parts. 'They're using you', I told him. 'Be careful. They're unscrupulous.' He redressed the balance in the second part of the interview, and we had a long discussion afterwards about precautions to be taken with the media. Edward Said's work was conceived at a time when the conflict between the different modes of representation still involved a stated – crushing – superiority of 'the West' over 'the Arab East'. It ended at a time when the East's response took a wrong turn. Torn between internal dictatorships and external diktats, the drive for liberation was held in a new kind of vice, between Islamism on one side, militarism on the other. Eight years after Said's death, insurrections in Tunis, Cairo, Bahrain, Libya and Syria have failed. Only Tunisia has done well. At least one hopes so. The other Arab countries have fallen back into the hands of dictators who are no less dangerous than those who went before – assuming they have changed at all. How would Said have formulated, paced and divided up his critique today? From what perspective? It seems likely that he would have reinforced his critique of Islamism. And perhaps he would have helped to create the word that English lacks to distinguish Islam from Islamism. His entire oeuvre suggests that he would not have abandoned his struggle against the self-satisfied hypocrisy of the West and its experts, who busily seek to cover up the enormity of their lie by examining tiny details, and that he would have highlighted the inseparable relationship between imperialism and the jihadist monster to which it gave birth. The element of paternity. One question remains definitively unanswered: Would he have given more space to the examination of those elements of the Quranic text that demand urgent reform and rigorous exegesis? Would he have agreed that, in the early twenty-first century, parts of the body of the Islamic world are affected by a serious illness and its immune system is at a low ebb? This does not mean giving ground – far from it – to those who, only yesterday, knew almost nothing about Muslim culture, and today fuel media headlines with bald, nonsensical statements such as, 'Jihad is a duty bequeathed by Muhammad to all Muslims'. These words by Alain Finkielkraut are neither false nor true, they are simply nonsense. First, they either ignore or fail to understand the fact that a word can mean different things, depending on context. 'Jihad' means the effort an individual makes to be a better person, just as much as any military effort or war. Second, not only do Finkielkraut's words mean nothing, they imply the dangerously mistaken idea that jihad is fundamental to Muslim dogma. Jihad is not one of the five pillars of Islam; it was not theorised in the Prophet's day, but appeared in treatises in the eighth century and after. It is true that more than one verse in the Quran calls for armed struggle in certain circumstances – these are among the verses urgently requiring a contextualisation that the religious scholars are tragically slow to provide. But to jump to the conclusion that every Muslim is required to fight against the same enemy in all circumstances, and that murderous Islamism is, ultimately, intrinsic to Islam as a whole, is a mark of both ignorance and irresponsibility. This apparent tautology contains much more than error: it is a flagrant manifestation of the damaging orientalism that Said so pertinently analysed and criticised. Not only does it bind all Muslims en masse to an intangible, fixed Islam but, more scornfully still, lowers the moral requirements where Islam is concerned. In other words, we'll allow them to be different by granting them an element of barbarity that reflects their cultural heritage.[1] Today, it is an easy matter to say that Said's argument in *Orientalism* lacked nuance; what was not easy – was in fact very hard – was to imagine and publish such a book at that time, given the degree of unconscious or 'good-natured' racism that served, and still serves, to consolidate that other, irreparable racism – the kind that is consciously full of hate.

Let us say that, having been born, like Edward, into two worlds at once, I can't help thinking of the repercussions of one world on the other, every time one of them fails to hear and understand what the other is saying. Particularly since these two worlds now largely inhabit the same space. I do part company with Edward to the extent that I don't understand things exclusively in terms of facts and content, but also, perhaps more, in terms of mental and temporal disconnect.

It is nonsensical to say that the Islamic State has nothing to do with Islam. To say that Islam sees itself in the Islamic State is more nonsensical still. What we are dealing with here is not an equivalence, but a lack of equivalence. This is the whole problem, and the reason why it is very unusual for anyone, however erudite – including Edward Said – to be able to say anything about it that is not approximate. For, as soon as the necessary things have been said to undo commonplaces, clichés and sweeping judgements, we have to deal with the other wave, which – while saying nothing different – does say something completely different. The Quran, however untranslatable – as it is in part – is indeed a text in which orders, threats and prohibition are frequent. In which women have an inferior status, whatever Islamic feminists may say, but also rights to protection that were considerable in the context of the time. Yes, nonbelievers – of which I am one – are unwelcome, to say the least. Every reader of the Quran has the right to find reasons to be dazzled by its language, drawn to its poetry, or deterred and even repelled by some aspect of the content of this extremely complex and contra-dictory text. But our reading does not exempt us from the need to reconcile critical thinking with a recognition of the irreplaceable element of a culture, memory or language. In saying this, I certainly do not want to fall in with a certain culturalism of the left, which is ready to abandon basic universal rights in the name of cultural specificity. I am trying to carve out a space that involves neither the denial of difference, nor regression negotiated in the name of difference. In her essay 'La double impasse', Sophie Bessis successfully deconstructs and criticises the functioning of this 'differentialism', which, on the pretext of respecting otherness, slides into a blindness that notably turns Islamism into 'the legitimate political horizon of Muslim Arab peoples, since, according to the intellectuals who espouse it, it is the only ideology produced by their own culture, reduced once again to religion, without external interference.'[2] In this regard, the Indigènes de la République in France are sadly exemplary. By slicing thought in two and using one half to destroy the other – tribe against tribe, race against race – their reaction against colonialism turns into a denial of history, obscuring what happened before and after colonisation. Their crusade against 'White people' and their use of 'us' and 'you' – the complete opposite of Said's approach – is an enterprise as watertight and compartmentalised as Said's was subversive, seeking to criticise the enclosure of thought through the use of the possessive pronoun. This all-or-nothing approach is a kind of intellectual monotheism, which views the social and political domains in terms of one truth, one God, one reading. It is the archetypal source of essentialism and the appropriation of the singular by the plural, the individual by the mass. Foucault put this 'single truth' in its place in the concluding words of his lecture at the Collège de France. 'What I would like to stress in conclusion is this: there is no establishment of the truth without an essential position of otherness; the truth is never the same; there can be truth only in the form of the other world and the other life.'[3] Said would have fully subscribed to this. Just as he agreed with Césaire and Fanon, when they inevitably talked of 'Black' and 'White', in order to dynamite the walls of foolishness and hatred erected by the world of one against that of the other. It stands to reason that those who still extol the virtues of colonialism, as Ernest Renan, Jules Romains and Roger Caillois once did, must be sent packing. The work of Edward Said in the 1970s had the great merit of providing an overview – at the level of thought and imagination – revealing the extent to which the racism of the past was still present. This racism is still present now. And this is precisely why it must be fought, not stoked. It is not enough to stir the vocabulary of Fanon, Césaire and Genet, unreviewed and unfiltered, into a magic potion. It is true that racism and colonialism, in Israel to begin with, have not yet finished doing damage. But, to fight them, we cannot apply a veneer of language that takes no account of change and the contemporary period. To fight against female genital mutilation is not to insult the black race. A battle that is not about 'Whites' is still worth fighting. Yes, Daesh is a phenomenon related to the Gulf wars. Yes, Bush and Blair should be brought before the International Court of Justice. But no, we can't dismiss the issue of Islamism in a phrase or a set of words. In the locked-down language of the Indigènes de la République, even women lose their rights to protection under the law. To equality. Seen from their end of the telescope, the castration of men within Islam was a consequence of racism, which is a corollary of colonialism. That's all there is to it. There's nothing more to think. There was no precolonial obscurantism in the Arab-Islamic world. The issue of virility, patriarchal power and the separation and inequality of the sexes is raised only in terms of colonialism. It is not also a cultural, social or religious phenomenon. So, all we need do is wait for the liberation of indigenous peoples humiliated by 'white' people, and we can pick up the liberation of women on the way out.

Responding, in the context of relations between dominators and dominated – central to Said's thought – raises a question of tone that is not simple to answer. Nor is it secondary. It can happen that an argument is accepted or rejected simply for reasons of tone. Tone involves the body. And a power relation. It has volume, more or less weight. Assurance. Aggressiveness, seduction and power. It determines the respective positions of the self and the other. And that other may change between the beginning and end of a sentence. Edward's work, pioneering in more than one domain, constantly had to improvise a voice and tone. With the passing of years, he came to master the art of using both, to intimidate and to enthral. His musical ear was a great help. Aside from his famous use of counterpoint, he also had a sense of prelude, cadence, notes of caution, variation, pauses, tempo, crescendo and leitmotiv. Inseparable from his intellectual training, his musical education taught him how to project his voice beyond university lecture theatres. When he was wrong-footed by others, he would lose the rhythm (unless the 'others' were friends or family). His tone would become more biting; controlled irony would veer towards sarcasm. We cannot remind ourselves too often that, nine times out of ten, the abuse of intelligence is an error of tone. Edward was happy to say the same thing in a different tone, but politically he said the same thing, no matter who he was talking to. This did a great deal for his credibility. 'He was critical of everyone', said Barenboim, 'he was always exactly the same with everyone.'[4] Edward's relationship to music did not stop there. Barenboim went on, 'The true intellectual must have the courage to focus on every tiny detail more carefully and persistently than the detail itself requires . . . In music you can't create a great work unless each specific little step works.'[5] Obsessed by detail and precision, Said was working on two fronts at the same time. On the one hand, racism, colonialism and the superiority claimed by one people, class or skin colour over another, where nothing could be allowed through. On the other, the relationship to the self and the other, requiring a different kind of rigour and lucidity, rooted in a basic degree of solitude and aptitude for exile. When the former voice silences the latter, humour, otherness and even the rights of love take a hit. When the latter dominates at the expense of the former, it often leads to cowardice, capitulation and the opportunism that attracts honours at the expense of honour. It was with a voice combining both aspects that Fanon wrote the conclusion to *Black Skin, White Masks*. This is a particularly fine piece of writing because it rises above both, and also rises above the enemy. Within it, thought and politics, inside and outside, are in tune. Here it is. Edward would undoubtedly not have argued with my including it in this book.

In this world, which is already trying to disappear, do I have to pose the problem of black truth?

Do I have to be limited to the justification of a facial conformation?

I as a man of color do not have the right to seek to know in what respect my race is superior or inferior to another race.

I as a man of color do not have the right to hope that in the white man there will be a crystallization of guilt toward the past of my race.

I as a man of color do not have the right to seek ways of stamping down the pride of my former master.

I have neither the right nor the duty to claim reparation for the domestication of my ancestors.

There is no Negro mission; there is no white burden.

I find myself suddenly in a world in which things do evil; a world in which I am summoned into battle; a world in which it is always a question of annihilation or triumph.

I find myself – I, a man – in a world where words wrap themselves in silence; in a world where the other endlessly hardens himself.

No, I do not have the right to go and cry out my hatred at the white man. I do not have the duty to murmur my gratitude to the white man.

My life is caught in the lasso of existence. My freedom turns me back on myself. No, I do not have the right to be a Negro.

I do not have the duty to be this or that . . .

. . . The disaster of the man of color lies in the fact that he was enslaved.

The disaster and the inhumanity of the white man lie in the fact that somewhere he has killed a man.

. . . I, the man of color, want only this:

... That it be possible for me to discover and to love man, wherever he may be.

The Negro is not. Any more than the white man.

... Superiority? Inferiority?

Why not the quite simple attempt to touch the other, to feel the other, to explain the other to myself?

Was my freedom not given to me then in order to build the world of the *You*?

My final prayer:

O my body, make of me always a man who questions![6]

In the late 1980s, in his book on Islamic art, Lebanese poet and calligrapher Samir Sayegh wrote, 'The mosque is by definition a museum of Islamic art.'[7] He went on:

Given that Islamic art is an art that ensures the relationship between the world and the beyond, rather than an art of creation destined to become a trace, we find it in ourselves, in going from the mosque to our home, from home into the street, from the street to the city, from the city to the whole Ummah. So that the real museum of Islamic art is life itself.

Life is also the orality that occupies a major place in Islamic culture. Minute by minute, treasures of inventiveness, knowledge and imagination are verbally deployed and go up in smoke, in a part of the world where private speech is the ever-present antidote to the speech of politicians and the media. The former usually stirs up life, the latter often death. One is as capable of poetry and humour as the other generally lacks both. What people say to others or to themselves forms an anonymous, inestimable heritage, free in the same way as hospitality. The role of orality in the writing of Arabic texts can never be overstated, starting with the Quran. My friend Oussama Salam, the child of two Lebanese Sunni families who played a historic role in the country, recently said to me, 'Arab rulers have prostituted speech. They have promised everything and delivered nothing. They have created such frustration that the mosque has become the last refuge where people can speak and put themselves in God's hands, where men's have failed them.' The movement Sayegh described, from mosque to house to street to the whole community, has gone into reverse. The community, street and house have gradually closed up like an accordion. They have given part of their life, movement and mobility to the one space of religion. To the point where the first decades of the twentieth century, which were marked by a liberation of the imagination and a proliferation of projects, gradually crumbled under the effects of repeated external intrusions and diktats and of internal defeat and powerlessness. Hypocrisy, boredom, brutality and censorship infected the language. The room for manoeuvre dwindled, and with it humour, which is not, to put it mildly, the strong point of religions.

As Tunisian storyteller and filmmaker Nacer Khemir says, 'The Arabs are shaped by two texts that are totally contradictory and equally fundamental: the Quran, which says what human beings must be, and the *Thousand and One Nights*, which says how they would like to live.' To conceive of Arab-Islamic culture outside this paradoxical back-and-forth – which is more fluid and oxygenated in some historical periods than in others – is to make a big mistake. The work that remains as yet largely undone – grounded in the Arabic language, which is the seedbed of this ambivalence – involves looking at this double life of thought and imagination. Its fecundity when times are favourable, and its terrible sterility when it sacrifices one side to the other – the freedom to dream to submission to dogma. The shock of the foundation of the state of Israel in 1948 caused a huge crisis in the imagination of the past and future, in the psychological economy of desire and taboo, profane and sacred. In these conditions, Said wrote, 'for the Arabs to act knowingly was to *create* the present, and this was a battle of restoring historical continuity', the role of the engaged writer then being 'to guarantee survival to what was in imminent danger of extinction'.[8] 'If before 1948 the Arabic novel could be described *sui generis* as a novel of historical recapitulation, then after 1948 it became a novel of historical and social development' in which was played out 'the near-tragic conflict between a protagonist and some "outside" force'.' Discussing the Palestinian writer Kanafani, Said describes a feeling that echoes that of his own trajectory: 'Like the land he left, his past seems broken off just before it could bring forth fruit.'[10]

> Unlike the Stendhalian or Dickensian case, the present is not an imaginative luxury but a literal existential necessity . . . That reality's intermittent nature, which in Mahfouz' postnaturalistic phase of the early sixties has been called *al-wujudiyah al-waqi'iyah* ('realistic existentialism'), developed more and more insistently into an aesthetic of minimalism and shattering effect; its complement was, I think, the quasi-Hegelian comic drama – or rather *dramatism*, since the play was in a sense the subject of the play – *Al-farafir* (1964) by Yousef Idriss.[11]

Throughout this chapter on Arabic prose after 1948, the year he turned thirteen, Said again finds something of himself in the work of others, in the form of an extremely precarious relationship to time. The dispossession of the land of Palestine is accompanied by mental dispossession, a hole that occupies and constantly eats away at the narrative core. We could add that the precipitate speed of history, around the creation of the nation states of the Arab world, severely accelerated and traumatised the time that had existed hitherto – the long, almost unmeasured time of Arab-Muslim culture. The time that unfolded in streets, courtyards, gardens and within the walls of a mosque, where children could play while their parents rested and prayed. From this point of view, I am in total agreement with Edward when he says that part of his Arabic culture is Muslim. Rather than a dialogue between religions, our aspiration should be an agreement between religions to stop interfering in the dialogue between people. In an interview Edward told his friend Tariq Ali, 'Friendships and intellectual and spiritual connections are far more important to me than the effects of my own identity. I don't have the time to waste on the idea of belonging to a national community.'[12]

XV

When our beliefs relate to our perceptions of our own survival, our relation to the self and the other is compromised. Our beliefs may be right or wrong; that is not the issue – or at least not the one I am exploring now. What I mean is that, when we equate reasoning with being right, we risk isolating ourselves. This isolation has reached tragic proportions in the Israeli–Palestine conflict. It has halted history. And thought. It has condemned both sides to stagnation and endlessly going back to zero – the complete opposite of inventive, musical repetition. The power to turn an enemy into a friend with a tone of voice, smile or glance, is something that the intellectual world dangerously abdicates. This failing particularly concerns me and, having experienced it, I am well placed to describe it. It was imposed on me by history, by my discovery, at the age of seventeen, of life in the Palestinian camps in Lebanon, while Israel, heavily armed both militarily and politically, scorned any idea of law with impunity, imposing its intrinsic superiority over us at every level. I have not changed my political opinions. Not at all. Israeli policy today is the epitome of lies and arrogance; it inspires nausea in me to see the indulgence it enjoys in the West, where anti-Semitism manifested itself with the greatest cruelty, leading to the horrors of Nazism. I haven't changed, but I have given myself permission to stop hating, to dismantle my compact image of the enemy and to make dialogue possible. Edward did too. And this 'permission' opened up extraordinary new directions. Nietzsche, in one of his most extraordinary essays, *On Truth and Lies in a Nonmoral Sense*, puts it like this:

> There are ages in which the rational man and the intuitive man stand side by side, the one in fear of intuition, the other with scorn for abstraction. The latter is just as irrational as the former is inartistic. They both desire to rule over life: the former, by knowing how to meet his principle needs by means of foresight, prudence and regularity; the latter, by disregarding these needs and, as an 'overjoyed hero', counting as real only that life which has been disguised as illusion and beauty. Whenever, as was perhaps the case in ancient Greece, the intuitive man handles his weapons more authoritatively and victoriously than his opponent, then, under favorable circumstances, a culture can take shape and art's mastery over life can be established.[1]

For my part – and thanks to a blow struck against reason by intuition – it is to the Israeli artist Ilona Suschitzky that I owe a trust and friendship that did not pass through any customs post of thought. Israel and Palestine were not banned from our relationship, but the most valuable element lay elsewhere. What is the most important step to take, in order to reconcile memories drawing on different sources and which are often contradictory? Choose sharing over persuasion – even leaving consistency behind, if the resulting 'distance' can aid vision. When the Israeli army bombed Gaza in 2009, Ilona and I took action, based on an understanding over and above the debates that might have held us back. With the help of our friends, we gathered hundreds of signatures for Barenboim's short statement, *Please listen before it is too late*. They came from all over the world and from all the arts, every sphere, beyond politics. What made me feel better was not so much the signatures flooding onto our screens from great musicians, architects, painters and writers, including some twenty Nobel Prize–winners. It was doing it with her, constructing a space, however provisional and fragile, that shed the tyranny of a past that stood there like a wall, obligatory as a duty. We would doubtless not have shared an analysis of the causes of the disaster, but what good would it have done to delve into our disagreements? There is nothing more liberating than to deprive rulers of the people they rule. I am certainly not saying that emotion can replace law, or that a longing for peace can replace the duty of resistance. What I am saying, to both myself and others, is that going forward is indissolubly linked to letting go. The letting go that happened between Ilona and me was comparable to what happened when Said met Barenboim. At the lowest point of his illness and chemotherapy, Edward only had to hear Daniel's 'hello' on the phone for his face to light up and his eyes shine, in anticipation of the pleasure of their conversation. Both men shared qualities of quickness and curiosity, with a great capacity for concentration and an awareness that time should not be wasted; in their friendship they maintained an almost perfect balance of difference and fellowship. They were brothers and equals. And this balance, orchestrated by music, was a first for Edward. Their relationship almost certainly helped loosen his defensiveness, without in any way making him less radical. In 1998, a year before the first meeting of Barenboim and Said's orchestra of Arab and Israeli musicians in Weimar, Said had condemned Garaudy and his negationist supporters in a ground-breaking article. First published in Arabic in the daily newspaper *Al Hayat*, and then in *Le Monde diplomatique*, this piece caused an outcry in Egypt. In that country, guilt at having signed a peace deal with Israel reinforced a sometimes blind intransigence among intellectuals. In their sclerotic world, Edward's opinion was inter-preted as an unacceptable concession to Israel. Far from simply maintaining his opinion, Edward restated it whenever the need arose. The story of this article began in Stockholm. Edward and I were there for a conference. Incapacitated by his treatment, he worked standing up, writing his weekly article for *Al Hayat*; meanwhile I was reading Saul Friedländer's book *Nazi Germany and the Jews*, which had come out the year before.[2] It so happened that, while at Éditions du Seuil, I had been given the job of launching Friedländer's book *When Memory Comes*. That was in 1978, shortly before the publication of *Orientalism*. The task was a huge problem for me. It caused me to have a nightmare in which I was forced to bleach my hair blond in order to exist. 'How am I going to promote a book by an Israeli Zionist?' I asked Le Seuil's director, Michel Chodkiewicz. I don't remember what he said. But I do remember that meeting Saul Friedländer in person put an end to my inner turmoil. 'What are you reading?' asked Edward twenty years later, busily writing with his back to me. I told him, and then flew into one of my fits of exasperated passion: 'We're hopeless! It's time that voices were heard in the Arab world, acknowledging the horror of the genocide against the Jews. It's time to end the indulgence that many intellectuals show for the negationists. Otherwise, what credibility do we have when we attack the policies of Israel?' The next day, in Göteborg, a fax machine delivered the pages Edward had sent for typing to his assistant Zaineb Istrabadi at Columbia. 'Here,' he said, 'this is for you.' It was the famous article that notably says:

> The idea that the Holocaust was simply a Zionist fabrication is doing the rounds in an unacceptable way. Why do we expect the whole world to recognise our sufferings if we are not capable of recognising the sufferings of others, even if they are our oppressors? Why, when we show ourselves to be incapable of dealing with facts that disturb the simplistic vision of right-thinking intellectuals who refuse to see the link that exists between the Holocaust and Israel? To say that we must recognise the reality of the Holocaust in no way means that we accept the idea that the Holocaust acquits Zionism of the wrong done to the Palestinians. On the contrary, recognising the history of the Holocaust and the insanity of genocide against the Jewish people makes us credible when speaking about our own history. It allows us to ask the Israelis and the

Jews to see the link between the Holocaust and the Zionist injustices imposed on the Palestinians. To go along with Roger Garaudy and his negationist friends in the name of freedom of expression is a stupid trick that will serve only to further discredit us in the eyes of the world. It's evidence of a fundamental misreading of history, a sign of incompetence and the incapacity to conduct a worthy fight.[3]

XVI

Edward was often drawn to authors and friends with opinions that differed from his own, even to the point of being antithetical. Not only did his admiration not necessarily include agreement with their views, he found the conflict between admiration and disagreement stimulating. Conrad was undoubtedly the most striking example in literature, but there were many others, including Kipling, Austen and Victor Hugo. To be precise, we should add that a dead enemy was more likely to merit his admiration. One that had lived. Genet, too, saved his admiration for the writing of 'enemy' authors, who embodied the France against which he struggled. 'Read the greats, read Gérard de Nerval and Chateaubriand,' he advised me, shortly after we first met. Knowing Cioran to be a friend of mine, he would ask me, mockingly, 'How's your Romanian rightist?' It would be hard to imagine two writers more politically opposed than those two. I wonder now what understanding can be gleaned from this pull in different directions. Why was I simultaneously friendly with two writers in French – Cioran and Genet – who were so distant from each other? Not forgetting that my friendship with Cioran, and then with his wife Simone Boué, went far deeper than my friendship and subsequent falling-out with Genet. Let me say it again, with Edward, the very construction of his thought required the compost, the raw material, of a 'beginning' grounded in duality. In an inner duel. This back-and-forth between him and the other was not that different from a back-and-forth between him and himself. The other had to be admirable in more than one way, in order to give excitement and meaning to the duel. We can say that Said neither could nor wanted to win his round against Edward at the latter's expense. In practice, his opponents and objects of criticism fell into two categories: those he admired and those he abhorred, which, to cut a long story short, went from Kipling to Bernard Lewis. Genet, meanwhile, needed to attack the enemy in his own language. What about me? It may be that my need to reconcile extremes – Genet and Cioran – reflected my twin identity as French and Lebanese. My French identity was more about the language than the people or the country. At that level, Cioran and Genet offered me more than I could ever have hoped for. They offered me two rich languages – those of the eighteenth and nineteenth centuries – in combination with two of the most marginal characters possible. Cioran gave me the means to laugh at the tragedy of Lebanon, while Genet enabled me to feel less politically alone. And that's not all. I think I have always been more astounded by the exercise of intelligence and imagination than by their finished products. Perhaps, to conclude, by their element of story.

It was through my friend François Bott that I had the opportunity to meet Cioran in 1977. Edward wanted to meet him. In 1968 he had written an article in *The Hudson Review* entitled 'Amateur of the Insoluble: On E. M. Cioran'. In it he said, 'Cioran, by his own admission, is "a *fanatic without convictions*", firmly, even hysterically committed to the amateurism of the insoluble. His prose is perfect for what it does, and it is airless as well: like the Europe he characterizes mercilessly, the prose becomes more interesting as it masters the art of surviving itself.'[1] Impressed by Cioran's darkness, by the elegance of his style, Said only half perceived his humour, which was not that of Wilde, Churchill or Guitry. It was not a *politeness of despair*, but its opposite. It was despair outraged, in both senses of the word, and delighted, in its unhappiness, to have hauled itself above the fray. The author of *Syllogisms of Bitterness* found energy in his pessimism, which he kept under constant surveillance, as hypochondriacs monitor their health. He had a unique way of cultivating the unsayable when it came to caricature. Of reaching the nuance of a nuance by way of extravagance. Cioran didn't laugh, he laughed at not laughing. The way he had of crying 'ha!' at the start or end of a phrase, of suddenly running a dishevelling hand through his impressive mass of grey hair, to reveal a face lit up, partly desolate, partly delighted by his desolation. To be, or not to be? Neither, he wrote. We can say that, for him, joy without a hint of disappointment was not joy at all. Cioran spoke as he wrote – on the one hand, he gave himself free rein; on the other, he used shortcuts. His prose had elements of anathema and prayer. It was lyrical and tormented. The result of the sifting of his excesses through the French language, 'a combination of straitjacket and salon'.[2] His words spilled out, his voice dragged, the combination of the two was irresistible. It was the rationed howling of a wolf. Dostoevsky's black humour shaped by Chamfort. 'French is snotty-nosed Latin', he confided, one immigrant to another, as we were walking across the Place des Invalides one day. Everything centred on his struggle with God, whom he could not dismiss without first invoking.

Edward and Cioran met at my home in Paris, in the early 1980s. Strangely, I no longer remember the content of the conversation. What I do remember is that their charm worked more on me than on each other. A few days later Cioran said dismissively, 'He's an intellectual.' Coming from him, the word was death. It betrayed an element of possessiveness, because he was possessive, and also conveyed the world that separated the two men. What is an intellectual, ultimately? It is impossible to say in a few words. Intellectual thought includes an element of will. Intellectuals want to understand the world, and to translate their thought into a kind of combat. This was clearly not true of Cioran, for whom the world was a wonderful illusion bound for destruction. It was true of Said. Between the two, my melancholy inclined me to my 'Romanian rightist', my passion and readiness for a fight towards my 'Palestinian leftist'. I was fully in step with Edward's political vision, profoundly out of step with Cioran's reactionary ideas. The author of *The Trouble with Being Born* brilliantly expressed the things that made me turn away from reality. Edward, the combative humanist, fuelled my desire for engagement, which dated from my childhood. He gave rigour and form to the energy that survived my suicidal instincts. What Cioran could not see was that Edward had a far greater tendency towards derision and reversal than was apparent, at first sight, in his words – which, I should say in passing, were not at all academic in the context of a conversation. The two men could never have challenged each other to a duel. They used different weapons. One killed at close quarters, with ardour and delicacy, the other at a distance, with a cold snigger. Cioran was a methodical destroyer, Edward a sceptical builder. Cioran had humour and irony on his side, Edward, irony first. Both knew that, ultimately, destruction and construction were the poor offspring of the two key verbs that mocked their intelligence: live and die. When Cioran took against someone or something, he didn't mince his words, but demolished his victim in a sentence. And he had undoubtedly taken against academic language. I remember his fury on hearing that the head of the philosophy and psychoanalysis department at Le Seuil had asked me about Nietzsche, before declining to give me a job, saying, 'What you have just said is correct and intelligent, but not conceptual enough.' 'Conceptual!! But that's unbelieeevably stupid!!' exclaimed Cioran in his inimitable Carpathian accent. All the same, Said was not, as Cioran thought, a knowledgeable expert; he was an amateur in the nineteenth-century sense. 'The particular threat to the intellectual today, whether in the West or the non-Western world, is not the academy nor the suburbs, nor the appalling commercialism of journalism and publishing houses, but rather an attitude that I will call professionalism.'[3] I don't think Cioran would have disagreed with this diagnosis. The cynicism of the Romanian was undoubtedly off-limits for the Palestinian, but they were still both, ultimately, 'amateurs of the insoluble'.

Cioran and Said had two contrasting visions of Paul Valéry, which encapsulate the improbability of their meeting of minds. Valéry makes a much-noted entry into Said's work in the first pages of *Beginnings*. At the point where he discovers the intoxicating potential of thought sustained by assiduous reading and work. 'Learning what I could from Valéry, I embarked on what I called a meditation on beginnings.' Valéry's love of precision and his very French refinement undoubtedly exerted their charm on Said, at a time when his own work was just beginning. Later, unlike most of his other travelling companions, this writer obsessed with 'the life of the mind' gradually disappeared from his field of vision. Why? Almost certainly because Edward no longer needed this intelligence that was absorbed by itself, in order to enjoy his own. Valéry's freedom from cynicism, which attracted Said, is what Cioran lambasts in him. More precisely, Said's cynicism is not the same as Cioran's. For Said, cynicism is an infringement of the basic rules of morality. For Cioran, cynicism is negative only when it serves an argument that ignores inner turmoil and torment. So, he skewers Valéry, having first cited him: 'I confess I have made my mind into an idol, but I have found nothing else that would serve.'[4] Valéry never got over the astonishment that the spectacle of his own mind caused him. He admired only people who made idols of their minds, and whose aspirations were so excessive that they could only be either fascinating or disturbing. Later, in relation to Mallarmé's megalomania, Cioran goes on:

> Valéry imitates and extends him, when he speaks of that *commedia* of the intellect he intended to write some day. The dream of excess leads to absolute illusion. When, on November 3, 1897, Mallarmé showed Valéry the corrected proofs of *Un Coup de dés* and asked him, 'Don't you find this an act of madness?,' the madman was not Mallarmé but the Valéry who, in a fit of sublimity, would write that in the strange typography of that poem the author had attempted 'to raise a page to the power of the starry heavens'.[5]

This piece was published in 1970, when Cioran was still known only to a handful of informed readers, while Mallarmé and Valéry were revered. We can guess how much the Romanian expatriate enjoyed excoriating these two French idols, elegantly demolishing a writer whom he did not admire enough to worship, but sufficiently to discuss him in some unforgettable passages. Conversely, in *Beginnings*, Said shows great admiration for both Mallarmé and Valéry. In his view, their works contained the signs of modernity – a mixture of irregularity and eloquence. In reality, Cioran and Valéry had much in common, including lucidity, a sense of concision and a lack of illusion in regard to what Valery called 'life, that glimpse'. Their difference was a matter of temperament, perhaps even of temperature. One was a hothead, the other was cool-headed. One threw himself physically into his words, making a pyre of them, the other remained outside them. According to Cioran:

> Only a maniac of lucidity could savor this cynical reversion to the sources of the poem, contradicting all the laws of literary production, this infinitely meticulous premeditation, these outrageous acrobatics, from which Valéry drew the first article of his poetic credo. He erected into a theory and proposed as a model his very incapacity to be a poet naturally. He bound himself to a technique in order to conceal his congenital lacunae; he set – an inexpiable offense! – poetics above poetry.[6]

With these words, he finishes off the wounded adversary he had earlier pretended to treat. I can't count the number of times I have binned attempts at aphorisms and poems, simply on remembering Cioran's voice describing a piece of writing as 'obnoxiously poetic'. His way of pronouncing the words, turning them into a cry, left an indelible mark. I can hear Edward saying, 'What does this have to do with your book, of which I am the unfortunate subject?' I shall try to reply. The further I go with the present essay, the more digression seems the best way for me to remain free. To escape paraphrase. Not to talk about his subjectivity, while camouflaging my own. To do what we did when we were together – use our closeness to make associations and connections, to find connections between subjects that were seemingly unrelated. To profit from their friction. I prefer the movement of the sea to straight lines.

XVII

Conrad, Proust, Swift, Vico, Dostoevsky, Foucault, Camus, Fanon, Orwell, Cioran, Valéry . . . the path this book is taking resembles our garden walks. City gardens. Edward was only moderately keen on nature. He liked to see it through a car window, and he liked to stop for a day or two in the country. But not to live there. He liked the sea. His relationship to exile and his relationship to culture went hand in hand. One without the other was not an option. He was happy in places that bore the imprint of human minds and hands. He didn't like flags, property or nationalism. He liked things that change, develop and emphasise singularity, uniqueness and mixing. Hybridity. He liked bookshops and concert halls. I wrote him a poem – 'gardens have been our houses' – of which I've just found a draft in a notebook, dated November/December 2000. At that time, I was living in New York, in a furnished apartment where I would wait for him to have a free moment, while working on my book of conversations with Green. Among the flood of 'obnoxiously poetic' phrases were these, which I do not repudiate: 'You gave me Bach, Swift and Conrad, with words so precise and pure that my head, panicked by the blur it was born with, retained the thread only at the price of a silent loss.' I had originally written, 'a hurtful loss', then crossed it out. 'No matter how much I told you to *look!* your eyes gazed at the autumn with a dog's impassive indulgence for a bird.' 'I liked it when your smile, emptied of knowledge, renewed your face with an amazed tenderness . . . You gave me the happy madness of borrowing your life, in the way that, as a child, I would play at making the troubling gestures of a grown-up . . . You gave me moments of faith in which, with my head on your shoulder, which shuddered as you walked, I would catch God with my eyes closed, like sunlight . . . We did the hardest thing, we loved each other.' And, on the last page of the notebook, strange words that I only half understand: 'The low part in my thoughts goes to meet a man who carries my past in his arms.'

In *Reflections on Exile*, Said reviews the different social and political categories of exile, before adopting a less conventional, more personal approach mediated by Adorno. Edward looks at exile from all sides, from a social and political ordeal to an ideal position for thought, but he keeps the best for the end. This use of counterpoint, to which he laid claim and which every analysis of his work has highlighted, goes along with another, more or less tangible trait. Beyond geographical distance and contrasting points of view, it quietly negotiates the negative and positive aspects of his own relationship to the world. And behind this negotiation, the element that relates to a certain 'consensus of the left' and the element that is free to leave that consensus behind. I won't go so far as to say that duty bears more heavily on the former and pleasure on the latter. But I would say that Said is closest to himself whenever he looks at his subject in the light of a certain solitude. We see this when he highlights these words by the twelfth-century Saxon monk Hugh of St Victor:

It is, therefore, a great source of virtue for the practiced mind to learn, bit by bit, first to change about in relation to visible and transitory things, so that afterwards it may be possible to leave them behind altogether. The man who finds his home-land sweet is still a tender beginner; he to whom every soil is as his native one is already strong; but he is perfect to whom the entire world is as a foreign land. The tender soul has fixed his love on one spot in the world; the strong man has extended his love to all places; the perfect man has extinguished his.

These marvellous lines were often cited by Eric Auerbach, in exile in Turkey during the war, to transcend 'the limits of nationalism'. Thinking of them at a time when a referendum has just 'democratised' dictatorship in Turkey, placing all the powers in the hands of one man, Erdogan, makes them disturbingly contemporary. Edward experienced his status as a Palestinian American as the stepping stone towards a fundamentally universal conception of human beings. To get there, he was obliged by the open wound of his country of origin – Palestine – to keep making detours through confrontation and denunciation. Few western intellectuals have had to maintain such a complex, demanding and emotionally laden combat. Against Israeli nationalism, and rooted in a relationship to a particular religion, however secular, the battle he waged for Palestinian rights, without resorting to nationalism and against any identity along ethnic lines, was a real tour de force.

There is a relationship between exile and love in Edward's life. As there is in mine. Our country lived by not being a country, by being outside the world. It was a place where happiness occurred on the margins, inseparable from solitude, with the intoxication of existence as its only identity. We met in places of transition – airports, concert halls, hotels, hired cars. Places where there were books, trees, a fireplace and a piano. The sea. Gardens. The difference between us was that he had a country to go back to. I wanted no other. Our happiness would no doubt have lasted longer if it had been less great. If we had been less in love. I mean, if we had been more aware of having gone, having been, where we wanted to go. Without asking anything more of each other. Why, despite or beyond our complicity, did I want the other side of existence, the one I had fled throughout my life? The conventional side. The threat of boredom. That was the question Edward asked me, and which I calmly ask myself today. Why was my freedom not enough? Why did I want everyday life? I think we delude ourselves if we believe we can live without delusions. Not that I regret having left, returned, stayed and left again. But I am aware, if only through my desire to write these words, that radical lack of recognition is a suffering that pride cannot ease. Perhaps it even makes it worse. There is almost certainly a connection between pride in exile and pride in love. My friend Pietro Citati said something about this that made an impression on me: 'Pride can be a virtue when you're young, but it ages badly.' He was right. There always comes a time when our origins – a word Edward set to one side – catch up with us. I realise this in writing these words, in the house in Lebanon where I was born. I have come back here, as though my life had gone home without thinking, without asking my opinion. Like a dog. I remember the day we met up in this house, when I had only just recovered from my illness and his had just begun. He sat down at the piano and I listened to him playing Bach's Partita no.4, looking out of the window into the garden where I spent my childhood. We had met after ten years of separation, as though it had never happened. That day I realised the terrible, marvellous proximity between the memory of happiness and the threatened joy of the moment. It was no coincidence that the one writer for whom we had a common, deep appreciation, whose world we most shared, was Proust. He gave us the palette of nuances that we lacked in our letters, too keen as we were to hold each other, to keep each other, too caught up in passion. 'Is not absence, for anyone who loves, the most certain, the most efficacious, the most vivacious, the most indestructible and the most faithful of presences?'[1] This sentence from the author of *Time Regained* is one of many to which Edward and I would have fully subscribed. To say that Edward's links to reality, to institutions and a certain social consensus, were different from mine would be an understatement. I have always loathed the trappings of life in society. Institutions, titles, hierarchies, honours, the clichés of recognition and power. This phobia against human vanity is very probably related to pride. But, for me, it runs far deeper. For as long as I can remember being alive, I have felt an almost pathological *disconnection* from life's rules. I have always been prey to an irreconcilable contradiction, which placed me halfway between

Edward and Cioran, an instinctive rejection of codes and artificial remedies for the absurdity of appearances, and a fierce desire to fight against injustice, to stand up for the weak, the dispossessed – in other words, to change the world I didn't believe in. Or, rather, that I was prepared to believe in only in order to change it. Here, again, the figure of the double is not far away. Is it a coincidence that I discovered 'Edward double you Said' long before I decoded 'E double D E'? If he could read these words, he would mutter, 'Hey D, it was about time.' Our contradictions slotted into each other, with a magnetic power akin to magic. They even conquered the reason of André Green, that most rational of analysts, who, having fought to help me regain my autonomy, my independence from Edward, finally threw in the towel during a session, saying, 'It seems that for you two it's a matter of destiny.' These words came from him as a capitulation. There were two Edwards, just as there were two Ds. His movement, in love as in everything else, took the form of counterpoint, mine of waves. His comings and goings were marked by the pain of separation, but they were contained and orchestrated like music. Mine exposed me to explosions and fallout, to rocks.

XVIII

One of the most trying episodes of our relationship occurred in March 2001. I was going to Beirut to take part in a conference – 'Mémoire pour l'avenir' – for which my friend Amal Makarem was one of the organisers. I had persuaded the poet Professor Jamel Eddine Bencheikh, the psychoanalyst François Villa and the historian Pierre Vidal-Naquet to be speakers. I remembered the latter's course on ancient Greece as indisputably the best I had attended at the Sorbonne. It is no secret that he carried the appalling memory of his parents' arrest by the Gestapo, after which they were taken to Drancy, before being deported and killed in Auschwitz. He fought against torture in Algeria. He had joined forces with those who were seeking a fair solution for peace between the Israelis and Palestinians. His visit to Beirut had intellectual and moral meaning, underpinned by his own history. I learned that a world congress of Holocaust deniers was to be held in Beirut at the same time. Notorious anti-Semites. I wrote the following short statement, to be signed by Arab intellectuals hostile to this event: 'We Arab intellectuals are appalled by this anti-Semitic project. We draw the attention of the Lebanese and Arab public to this gathering and call on the Lebanese authorities to ban the holding of this unacceptable event in Beirut.' Fourteen signatures were collected in record time, including those of Adonis, Mahmoud Darwish and Edward Said. At that time, our relationship had broken down. So I asked my friend Eric Hazan to call Edward and ask him to sign. He immediately said, 'Yes of course.' This text and the names of the signatories were headline news in *Le Monde* of 16 March 2001. With the following details: 'On the initiative of two neo-Nazi negationist organisations, Vérité et Justice in Switzerland and the American Institute for Historical Review (IHR), a conference entitled "Revisionism and Zionism" is scheduled to take place 31 March–3 April in Beirut.' This article caused a stir. Jacques Chirac, the French president at that time, called his friend Rafic Hariri, the Lebanese prime minister. I don't know how the discussions went. What I do know is that the conference was banned. And that, a few days later, I was stunned, staggered, to learn that Edward had changed his mind and publicly stated that he disagreed with the call for a ban. In essence, he gave as his reason, 'I have always been against bans. Condemnation would have been enough.' Al Jazeera interviewed a woman who presented me as a manipulator, the message being that Dominique Eddé had forced Edward Said's hand. Watching the scene on television, Dina Haidar, who was a friend to both of us, instantly called Edward in New York, asking him to refute this calumny, stick to his principles and publicly retract his statement. Nothing came of it. Shortly before his death, Edward said on the phone, 'Forgive me D.' Perhaps he was right to think that it is not the intellectual's role to call for 'bans'. But that was not the issue. He should not have withdrawn his support. Hazan had told him what the statement said. He was wrong to retract. I have here a notebook, in which I jotted key points day by day. Notably the content of two phone calls. In relation to the 'ban', Elias Khoury, one of the signatories, who was in New York, said, 'You know that Edward's problem is not with the ban, it's with you.' Meanwhile, on hearing that the congress had been cancelled, Pierre Vidal-Naquet told me, 'This is a historic event.' In *Le Monde* of 18/19 March 2001, his friend Elie Barnavi, the Israeli ambassador, 'hailed the response of Arab intellectuals'. Vidal-Naquet asked if I'd like to meet him, I said no. Barnavi had been Sharon's ambassador and I wanted nothing to do with him. 'I understand,' replied Vidal-Naquet in a friendly way. His presence and understanding were a great help to me in dealing with Edward's 'betrayal'. Our relationship was hurt by this, but it was far from over. I loved him. We loved each other. We liked each other a bit less than before, but our love was just as strong.

XIX

Preparing for death is pointless. As is distancing yourself. The news of his death came over the phone. Devastating. Not being able to be with the one you love in his last days is an ordeal totally lacking in humanity. It was an ordeal that Edward had not imagined I would suffer. 'Tell her I will see her again,' he told our closest friend from his hospital bed, a few days before his death.

In the spring of 2004, I discovered Sedef Island, off Istanbul. A garden surrounded by sea. It was there that I decided at last to read *Nostromo*, the novel that held such a particular place in Edward's relationship to Conrad, his characters and himself. This book, seldom mentioned in his thesis on Conrad, takes up thirty-five crucial pages of *Beginnings*. He would return to it now and then, in later writing, and to the main character Gould – Said had two Goulds in his life – who is to Latin America something of what Kurtz is to Africa. 'Conrad saw Kurtz as a European in the African jungle and Gould as an enlightened Westerner in the South American mountains, capable of both civilizing and obliterating the natives; the same power, on a world scale, is true of the United States today, despite its declining economic power.'[1] If there is one work of fiction that illustrates the opposite of paraphrase, the invention of a world from beginning to end – echoing Said's questioning of the relationship between the Quran and fiction[2] – it is *Nostromo*. The country of Costaguana is a complete fictional construction, containing a multitude of human relationships that all converge like a spider's web towards a vision of humanity doomed to failure. Conrad's recurring theme – the corruption of ideals by money – is here multiplied to the nth degree. Charles Gould, heir to the Sulaco silver mine, is descended from a line of British expatriates. In him, as in Kurtz, betrayal is the cause of immeasurable moral collapse. Initially driven by the noblest feelings, Gould becomes a slave to his mine and the financial interests that come to dispossess and dominate him. 'There is no credulity so eager and blind as the credulity of covetousness, which, in its universal extent, measures the moral misery and the intellectual destitution of mankind.'[3] Impossible to sum up in a few lines, this extremely complex novel has two particularities, compared to the rest of Conrad's work: it is long – over five hundred pages – and it is set on solid ground. It shows the world of men as even harsher when it is cut off from its unconscious background, from sailing and fluid horizons. In the light of *Nostromo*, my question concerning the author of *Culture and Imperialism* is, why did he not more clearly see, or at least emphasise, Conrad's merciless critique of capitalism? The quotation above is the only time it is stated, and in few words. Yet Conrad's always radically critical vision of money and capitalism is just as striking as his acceptance of imperialism without illusions. It is true that his ferocious, premonitory vision of the triumph of finance is never transformed into any kind of militancy. Conrad is neither for nor against the world he describes, he simply observes it. And, to the extent that he does not believe in collective battles – in his eyes, they are all bound to degenerate under the effects of human greed and cruelty – he remains within the narrow, rigorous margin of observation. This is a choice Said decided not to make. He chose to use his will in service of collective action. It is almost certainly because it did more to disarm him than to sustain his fight that he says little of Conrad's vision of capitalism, which was concerned with human nature, rather than socialism and Marxist anticapitalism. Psychologically evident novelistic elements could not be exported wholesale into the world of ideas. Said's thought was concerned with progress – officially, at least.

Powerlessness, an ever-present threat, might appear as an unavoidable fact when reviewing a situation, but never in the time of action. Generally speaking, it is fascinating to note the place of subjectivity in intellectual work, including when that work is most careful not to sacrifice paradox to a thesis. Fascinating, too, to see the extent to which Said's relation to Conrad involved signals of recognition[4] – affinities, disagreements, things said and not said, conscious and unconscious elements – all ultimately leading to the gates of death, to the same vision of a humanity betrayed by itself, irreconcilable. Nostromo is an Italian sailor turned captain of *cargadores*, who, with the help of French aristocrat Decoud, undertakes to guard the mine's treasure, which comes under threat when the political power of the Blanco party is overthrown by Pedro Montero, and chaos ensues. The treasure is taken to Great Isabel island, where Decoud, ravaged by loneliness and pessimism, takes his own life. This leaves only Nostromo, the man of many qualities, who loses them all in falling prisoner to money. His real treasure, his wife Emilia, is abandoned and sacrificed. The infernal chain of events arising out of the triumph of greed – at the exorbitant cost of love and freedom – proves fatal to all. Published in 1904, this novel was strikingly contemporary in political terms. Conrad, who died between the wars in 1924, rejected the figure of the hero in favour of the man overwhelmed by his sickness. Finding himself in possession of everything and every power, 'our man', on whom all hopes rested, becomes possessed in turn by what he has and by his powers. 'Nevertheless,' writes Said, 'in part 1 Nostromo is allowed an extraordinary moment of beautiful, unspoiled freedom. To my mind it is the most splendidly theatrical moment in all of Conrad's fiction.'[5] Nostromo's vision of the 'beginning' is what Said sought to renew throughout his life. Not condemning it to fail, while recognising its element of illusion. He summed it up as follows: 'The moral of such a conception is that the fabric of life is manufactured by some devilish process the purpose and logic of which is profoundly antihuman.'[6] Here lies the narrow, definitive gap between their two visions.

Conrad's favourite opera was Bizet's *Carmen*. The two operas most reflecting Said's obsessions were Mozart's *Così fan tutte* and Beethoven's *Fidelio*. Both Conrad and Said share an element of ambivalence in their depiction of women. The great difference is the figure of *Fidelio*, which does not exist in Conrad's work. The three operas I have just mentioned are all about women as seen by men, their capacity to switch – in Bizet and Mozart – and their capacity for faithfulness and devotion in Beethoven. Love is seriously wounded in Conrad's universe. It is as distant, unattainable, even cold, as the landscapes of his childhood in exile in Russia. A woman is particularly desirable if she is silent, like Hermann's niece in *Falk*, whose eponymous character was rumoured to have 'won his wife at cards with the captain of an English ship', and Alice, daughter of Alfred Jacobus the ship-chandler, in *A Smile of Fortune*.[7] Here, I can't help associating Conrad's fantasy of the woman who doesn't speak with something Edward confided to me about a woman with whom he had had an intense sexual relationship. He said, 'I could never understand why she didn't speak. Not once. She was splendid and silent.' It sounded like one of Conrad's short stories. And as I remained puzzled and silent, he went on. 'What do you think? Why that silence?' I didn't have the presence of mind to turn the question round and ask him why her silence had served eroticism so well. I preferred to remind him that the power of speech had a formidable power of dissuasion. Here, again, in the two interchangeable, manipulated couples of *Così fan tutte* and Leonore's boundless love for Florestan, captive of the ferocious prison governor Don Pizarro in *Fidelio*, we find Said and his double. His story, or the complex variations of his emotional and psychological life. His capacity for love and switching. His irony, verging on betrayal, and his innocence, verging on the childlike. His grasp of both. Leonore disguised herself as a man called Fidelio in order to get into the prison, work there and, ultimately, free Florestan, having involuntarily, dangerously won the heart of the jailer's daughter Marzelline, who falls in love with 'him'. I'm not suggesting that the libretti of these two great operas had the same power of attraction for Said as their music, which is far superior. He never stopped saying and writing so himself. Nevertheless, he did discuss them a great deal. Furthermore, Fidelio's happy ending bothered Edward, who found the liberation and reuniting of Leonore and Florestan too 'easy'. He would have preferred a more complicated, less happy ending. I think he even whispered the idea to Barenboim. For Said, as for Conrad, a conflict settled was only ever one less knot, a temporary denouement.

I wonder, ultimately, whether writing is not a way of putting death to the test. Of not coming to terms with it. Of not coming to terms with the fact of coming to terms with it. In other words, of reinforcing life on its vulnerable border with the past and death. Drawing from the present – the last bit of current life – the impulse that swings back and forth, linking the time before to the time ahead. 'All my goodbyes are said, but I come back again,' wrote Rilke. When, at the end of a life, the movement of goodbye merges with the content of writing itself, be it literature or music, it usually delivers the content of a thought or feeling in a state of extreme concentration, all the more durable for its awareness of threat. The more our physical forces dwindle, the harder this effort of back and forth, this convocation of presence through nothing but the allied forces of thought and love. From this point of view, Said's *On Late Style* was heroic. Consumed and exhausted by sickness, he still had the willpower not to allow time to collapse on him without his participation in its written version, in history. After we met in 1978, Edward recorded a music cassette for me, with two composers who seemed to me at the time to be total opposites, Mozart and Strauss. Mozart's Divertimento in D Major, Strauss's *Metamorphosen* and *Four Last Songs*. The Allegro of the Divertimento soon became the leitmotiv of our meetings, our happiness, the *Four Last Songs* that of a subterranean threat to which I clung, with a mixture of worry and melancholy, as I became familiar with it. The more I listened to them, the more I seemed to hear Jessye Norman sing of life after death. We were young; we could enjoy the luxury of a love that dances and ages at the same time. Reading Edward's writing on Strauss and Mozart forty years later, I can gauge the extreme continuity of his relationship to music and, through it, to time. In two consecutive chapters, 'Return to the Eighteenth Century' and '*Così fan tutte* at the Limits', he shows us how the start of the end of a cycle draws on the beginning, on its roots. In this case in the eighteenth century. How Richard Strauss returns to Mozart, to define new starting points in his own music. He cites Del Mar on the *Four Last Songs*: 'The tiredness of great age in the presence of impending and welcome death is not really sad but something far deeper. It is the prerogative of great art that it arouses nameless emotions which can tear us apart.'[8] And, having subjected Strauss to the critiques of Adorno and Gould, which he does and does not share, Said sums up his hearing of the composer's last works as follows: 'They are escapist in theme, reflective and disengaged in tone, and above all written with a kind of distilled and rarefied technical mastery that is quite amazing.' For additional evidence of this, a detail in relation to *Metamorphosen*, which is 'scored in twenty-three separate lines for as many strings.' Concluding with words that read like Edward's self-portrait:

> Perhaps the last thing one would normally say about Strauss's final works is that they are defiant, but I think that is exactly the word for them . . . Because a minimalist aesthetic is at work here, the music seems to stand aside: it renounces claims to metaphysical statement of the sort embodied in comparably eminent composers of the time, and it pliantly, agreeably, and immediately appears to an ear surprised, perhaps even shocked by the music's lack of complaint.[9]

I think that Edward too had prepared himself very early for his work to end with no metaphysical alternative, and no complaint at not having one. In so doing, he attained an economy and exactitude of writing much greater than in most of his previous work.

All things considered, his last writings were not unrelated to his piano interpretations which, focusing mainly on Bach, continued to gain in precision, despite the weakening of his physical strength. This precision brings us to a major musical and intellectual figure in Said's life and in the story of his thought: Glenn Gould.

In Said's eyes, Gould, who was born in 1932 and died in 1982, epitomised abstract brilliance and the investment of self, the intelligence of ideas and the understanding of sound, the highest point in the meeting of music and personality. With, as his main point of reference, Bach, the composer Edward regarded as without equal. He saw Gould as an ideal, a man who embodied music without abandoning thought, clarified but did not simplify it, reinvented it by reinventing the work of the pianist. Said wrote, 'His capacity to deploy an almost verbal intelligence through his fingers – each knowing how to act independently of the rest – set standards that no one has been able to emulate or match.'[10] Where fingers are concerned, Gould's and Said's were similar. The same finesse, length, dexterity, restlessness and autonomy. Listening to Edward playing one of the *Goldberg* variations or a prelude from *The Well-Tempered Clavier* also meant listening to him listening to Gould. He was transported by Gould, by his combination of control and freedom (both extreme), eccentricity and precision. This was what he, Said, aspired to at the intellectual level. Knowing that, whatever we do, in the domain of thought, we can never attain the qualities of concentration and pleasure that music permits. I wrote a little earlier that Edward avoided madness. He did not avoid Gould, in whom doctors diagnose a form of autism. The condition lodged in Gould's genius fascinated him. He wondered in fascination how this man, shut away in a hotel, awake at night, sleeping half the day, avoiding the world, taking all kinds of medication, achieved such dazzling mastery. There is almost no book of Edward's that doesn't mention Gould at one point or another. I also think that he was not only curious, but troubled in an admiring way, by the fact that Gould had decided so early to stop playing concerts. When Edward was in a concert hall, it was as though he were there with himself. He was united, or reunited. It was a time when his inner conflict stopped – his double was beside him, conquered, on the same wavelength as him. He did undoubtedly write a great deal, like Adorno before him, about the commercial nature of the music industry. About the loss suffered by art when it is made available to all, at the price of complexity. Nevertheless, the deeply bourgeois atmosphere of the concert hall suited him perfectly. Never quite settled anywhere, in that setting he was completely at home. From the entrance to the moment he found his seat, to the wait, the last glance at the programme – of which he had several interpretations in his mind – the arrival onstage of the musicians, the sound of the first note, he was safe. Physically, emotionally and intellectually attuned to himself, ready to let himself be overcome with wonder, a critique, or both at once. The architecture of the building, the interval, the human landscape, the place as an island in the city, the elegance of some, the quality of listening in others – everything related to a concert fitted him like a glove. This closed auditorium, containing the promise of a temporary miracle, was his homeland, wherever it was. After his death, it was some time before I could think of going there again. I broke my fast in Istanbul, with a concert at the home of my friends the Tütens. That night I dreamed these words: '*La musique, c'est du silence en fête*' (Music is the celebration of silence). If Edward understood why Gould had turned his back on concerts and his audience, he remained unsure about what he, Edward, thought about it. No doubt he secretly asked himself, what would I have done in his place? In terms of doubles, Gould was, in his eyes, the madness he had escaped and the genius he envied. The opposite of the other genius that is Barenboim, whom he admired without fear or envy. Barenboim pulled him back towards life.

XX

Names and dates had the greatest importance in Said's system of representation. There are passages of methodical enumeration, for example in *Out of Place*, that may seem puzzling. The same is true in *Covering Islam*, where the introduction is studded with secondary names alongside the major ones, and dates and titles of press articles that are usually confined to footnotes. In reality, the inclusion of detail is part of Said's originality. With the aid of his prodigious memory, he sprinkled his writings with prosaic details intended to bind the fabric, create texture and, crucially, to contain dispersal and anxiety; chronological and genealogical details served as safeguards for this adventurer who was 'not quite right', 'out of place'. In the case of *Così fan tutte*, dates were highly significant: first performed on 26 January 1790 – the day before Mozart's birthday and a year before his death – at the Burgtheater in Vienna, *Così fan tutte* was the first opera that Edward, then still a schoolboy, saw in the United States in the 1950s. When he wrote about this opera, he was at the end of his life, or in any case under serious threat of losing it. The meeting of two twilights – that of Mozart and Said writing about Mozart – is as rich in novelistic terms as the opera's libretto verges on farce, quite unlike the music which, however much it suits the roles, has valedictory tones of a depth that bears no relation to the superficiality of the characters. A more fascinating context for Edward is hard to imagine. Behind the instability and lack of gravity in the relationships involved (two couples manipulated by the rather perverse Don Alfonso, who, unlike Don Giovanni, escapes unscathed), he could detect, note by note, the extraordinary potential of musical maturity to undermine triviality. The warmth arising out of the cold. The resources of versatility when genius is involved. Supported by Mozart's letters to his wife, Constanze, who was taking a cure in Baden when he was writing *Così fan tutte*. In one of these letters Mozart appears annoyed with the opera's frivolity. In another from the same period, he tells Constanze how excited he is by the idea of seeing her very soon, adding the strangely contradictory words, 'To me everything is cold – as cold as ice.'[1] Other letters, says Said, 'characterize his special combination of unstilled energy (expressed in the sense of emptiness and unsatisfied longing that increases all the time) and cold control: these qualities seem to me to have a particular relevance to the position of *Così fan tutte* in his life and oeuvre.'[2] Who is Don Alfonso? An actor, a teacher, an educated man, a plotter, a courtier, a man of great sexual experience who, at this point in his life, wants to control the experience of others. This is more or less the portrait of him that Said paints, before adding that, beyond the comedy of the character, he embodies many personalities of the cultural world of Mozart's time.

> To have discovered that the stabilities of marriage and the social norms habitually governing human life are inapplicable because life itself is as elusive and inconstant as his experience teaches makes of Don Alfonso a character in a new, more turbulent, and troubling realm, one in which experience repeats the same disillusioning patterns without relief.[3]

Said also repeats – three times – the same or almost the same words concerning the feeling of painful emptiness and cold control felt by Mozart. A feeling that was familiar, to say the least, to the author of *On Late Style*, particularly in the year leading to his death. 'Listening to the aria and seeing the hubbub of serious and comic elements jostling one another on the stage, we are kept from wandering off into either speculation or despair, obligated to follow the tight discipline of Mozart's rigor.'[4] Here, again, in Said's late look at a late work by Mozart, we find the pessimism of intelligence challenged – with less margin than before – by the optimism of the will. 'Mozart never ventured closer to the potentially terrifying view he and Da Ponte seem to have uncovered of a universe shorn of any redemptive or palliative scheme, whose one law is motion and instability expressed as the power of libertinage and manipulation, and whose only conclusion is the terminal repose provided by death.'[5]

At the end of his life, Edward came up against a hard core that resisted his immense effort to tie up every loose end. At both the political and existential levels. This resistance to his powerful desire for synthesis he termed 'irreconcilability'. The phenomenon is comparable to the one he describes in relation to the Beethoven's late work. In *Parallels and Paradoxes*, Said said to Barenboim, 'There's something irreconcilable about it, in some way. In other words, instead of getting resolutions, you're getting things being pulled apart.'[6] And it was no coincidence that, in his book *Freud and the Non-European*, he made a connection between the *Late Quartets* and *Missa Solemnis* of Beethoven and Freud's *Moses and Monotheism*. On Moses he writes, 'Everything about the treatise suggests not resolution and reconciliation . . . but, rather, more complexity and a willingness to let irreconcilable elements of the work remain as they are: episodic, fragmentary, unfinished (i.e. unpolished).'[7] This was also true of him as a man of political engagement when, having shed his burden of persuasion (the work was done) to become just a man fighting illness, he considered the 'intransigence, difficulty and unresolved contradiction'[8] of coming to conclusions.

The first period of our relationship began when the French translation of *Orientalism* was first published in France, the second with the publication of *Culture and Imperialism* in 1993. This was a time when his desire to live, create and love was at its height, despite the leukaemia that had him repeating that he was 'a dying man', as though to bounce back all the better. It is only now, rereading these two books, that I see the relationship between them and us. Edward came back to me, as he came back to the first of these two books in writing the second. Repeating or returning to a theme in a new movement was a striking characteristic of his life and work. At both the emotional and intellectual levels, all his departures – he hated departures – were instinctively accompanied by a promise to start again. We sometimes played a modified version of consequences. One of us would write a question, fold down the paper, and the other would write a reply without knowing the question. Not long ago I found a paper napkin on which I had written, 'What is love?' and he had replied, 'The best is return and recapitulation.'

In a letter of December 1981, Edward sent me two verses from a poem by Wallace Stevens – 'Mozart, 1935'.

> That lucid souvenir of the past,
> The divertimento;
> That airy dream of the future,
> The unclouded concerto . . .
> The snow is falling.
> Strike the piercing chord.
>
> Be thou the voice,
> Not you. Be thou, be thou
> The voice of angry fear,
> The voice of this besieging pain.

Thirty-five years later, I have found the entire poem, with the following lines that he had deliberately left out, and with good reason.

> We may return to Mozart.
> He was young, and we, we are old.
> The snow is falling
> And the streets are full of cries.
> Be seated, thou.[9]

What world were we dreaming of, Edward and I? I couldn't exactly say. I think that, beyond our relationship, we never confused dream with reality. Our battles against injustice, domination, colonialism and unbridled capitalism were rooted in a representation of the world that showed far more clearly what we didn't want, than what we did. We were bourgeois rebels, opponents of the established order, rather than revolutionaries. Purity frightened us both. In passing, I should say that I'm not sure, reading his piece on Genet, that Said gauged the full extent of Genet's use of purity in *The Criminal Child*, of death's invasion of life in the name of purity. It takes nothing from his genius as a writer, but a little from his political 'credibility', to which, moreover, he laid no claim. Generally speaking, I do not believe that human criteria divide along strictly political lines. In the context of our causes, Genet was undoubtedly a better political friend than Camus. But to conclude that, compared to Genet, Camus was a 'frightened, finally ungenerous mind' is a step I am not prepared to take.[10] Genet's courage and sense of solitude were undoubtedly exceptional. Camus' humanism, deficient for the reasons we have seen in relation to the Arabs, was no less real and, in many ways, generous. The sense of irony that was so important to both Edward and me put us instinctively on our guard against happy endings that are constructed in a brain behind closed doors. He preferred to describe himself as engaged, rather than militant. Being more anarchistic and marginal, less solid and balanced than him, I preferred, then as now, to avoid definitions. Our situation necessarily exposed us to idiosyncratic pontificators; he escaped this better than I, since he never stopped feeding and increasing his intellectual capital, turning it into a reference point, a gift to thought, although – and happily – unclassifiable in a few words. The recurrent wars and massacres in our countries – Palestine and Lebanon – and then those of Iraq, with their appalling consequences, constituted the macabre world in which our resistances were constructed and/or exhausted – a world at the centre of which we made room for love and beauty. From where it became easier to face the enemy, starting with Israel, without flinching, without making the concession that betrays the essential, and without sliding into hatred. Rejecting all the political and media accommodations underpinning agreements made between the powerful to the detriment of the Palestinian people, the position represented by Said was exemplary. Historic. I was proud to be so close to him during this time, when he embodied such rigour, courage and solitude.

XXI

I don't feel strong enough to go over each of the essays in his collection *The Politics of Dispossession*, published in 1994. They form a coherent set that is one of the keystones of his work. Why do I not have the strength? Not due to disagreement, of course, but to fatigue. The twenty-five years since that book was published have brought such a chain of defeats and disasters in the region, that people of my generation have run out of words and breath to sort and distinguish one loss or massacre from the next. Said's political work is historic in terms of both thought and the events it records: it archives for future generations that point in history when Islamism, though not yet triumphant, had set dangerously to work, notably through Hamas, and the Israeli authorities were supporting it, to further weaken the Palestinian Authority, while blindly, methodically devastating the living conditions of the Palestinians. In this book he writes,

> The question to be asked is how long can the history of anti-Semitism and the Holocaust in particular be used as a fence to exempt Israel from arguments and sanctions against it for its behavior toward the Palestinians, arguments and sanctions that were used against other repressive governments, such as that of South Africa. How long are we going to deny that the cries of the people of Gaza . . . are directly connected to the policies of the Israeli government and not to the cries of the victims of Nazism?[1]

Edward Said argued for the creation of a single state, in which Israelis and Palestinians, condemned to live together, would transform that challenge into a unique experiment. In the tradition of thinkers such as Hannah Arendt, Judah Magnes and Martin Buber, who argued between the wars for the creation of a two-nation state, Said took up the cause of the one-state solution in the 1990s. In an essay entitled 'The One-State Solution' he concludes,

> The alternatives are unpleasantly simple: either the war continues (along with the onerous cost of the current peace process) or a way out, based on peace and equality (as in South Africa after apartheid) is actively sought, despite the many obstacles. Once we grant that Palestinians and Israelis are there to stay, then the decent conclusion has to be the need for peaceful coexistence and genuine reconciliation. Real self-determination. Unfortunately, injustice and belligerence don't diminish by themselves: they have to be attacked by all concerned.[2]

These few lines could be read as wishful thinking, were they not part of a complex argument that recognises both peoples and, crucially, a now ineluctable reality on the ground: separation is no longer physically possible, given both the colonisation of the West Bank and Jerusalem and the high proportion of Israeli Arabs (over twenty per cent). This viewpoint is shared by Eric Hazan and Eyal Sivan who, in their book *Un État commun: Entre le Jourdain et la mer*, observe that, if the territory were divided, the borders would be entirely controlled by the Israelis, penning the Palestinians into fragmented territories contained within Israel.[3] Like Said, they note that the cohesion of Israel is maintained by the state of war, and would deteriorate once the tension was reduced. And they conclude, with impeccable logic, that war cannot be a project in itself, one that replaces the search for a solution. In his argument in favour of one state for two peoples, Said cites at length the Israeli historian Zeev Sternhell, who identifies the missing link in the Zionist argument. Its hole. Sternhell writes,

Contrary to the claim that is often made, Zionism was not blind to the presence of Arabs in Palestine . . . Neither the Zionist movement abroad nor the pioneers who were beginning to settle the country could frame a policy toward the Palestinian national movement. The real reason for this was not a lack of understanding of the problem but a clear recognition of the insurmountable contradiction between the basic objectives of the two sides. If Zionist intellectuals and leaders ignored the Arab dilemma, it was chiefly because they knew that this problem had no solution within the Zionist way of thinking.[4]

For my part, I think that we can never focus too much on this intentional dead end, which has tainted all political arguments over the last six decades. Through annexations, occupations, and the rape of the physical and mental territory, Zionism, as a prisoner of its contradictions, has constantly driven the Palestinians into exile or into a corner. It has insisted on creating – or trying to create – a situation on the ground that moves and deports both arguments and populations. With massive support from foreign powers, it has produced an extremely effective rhetoric, in which the chronological order of events in Palestine has been systematically shattered by the logic of a different history and geography – that of western anti-Semitism and the Nazi genocide. The result is that the narratives of the two peoples, Israeli and Palestinian, have become irreconcilable (this word comes back on a loop in Said's last writings). In 'The One-State Solution' he says,

I see no other way than to begin now to speak about sharing the land that has thrust us together, sharing it in a truly democratic way, with equal rights for each citizen. There can be no reconciliation unless both peoples, two communities of suffering, resolve that their existence is a secular fact, and that it has to be dealt with as such.

This does not mean a diminishing of Jewish life as Jewish life or a surrendering of Palestinian Arab aspirations and political existence. On the contrary, it means self-determination for both peoples. But it does mean being willing to soften, lessen and finally give up special status for one people at the expense of the other.

It goes without saying that the idea of a mixed state founded on openness and exchange, the end of walls and barbed wire, is the only one worth dreaming of in human and political terms. Let us say it is an ideal. But is that not precisely its stumbling block? Can it be realised? Can it move from the abstract to reality and, instead of remaining an ideal, turn into a utopia? I remember the harsh words of a woman whose courage I admire, the Israeli dissident Amira Hass. What she said to me, in essence, was that peace is not a formula you can choose, like a product in a supermarket. It is true that the degradation of the situation – now overlaid by the rise of Islamism, and actively assisted by Israeli governments – leaves little room for a project of coexistence and little desire on either side. As professor Karim Bitar recently told me, 'If this process ever happens it can't but take the form of a long path of suffering.' And then, at the nerve centre of the conflict, is Jerusalem, a place that is quintessentially irrational. As long as the major powers give way to Israel on this issue, there will be thousands if not millions of people, both inside and outside the territory, who are ready to get themselves killed, with others, for what they regard as a 'holy place'. The internationalisation of the city, the solution advocated by Germaine Tillion, remains the only one that can ensure peace. It would 'tangentially' have the advantage of including Christians in the peace process. Because, in advocating a shared state, people tend to forget that, by the same token, the most ancient populations – Christians in Iraq and Palestine, Copts in Egypt – are driven to the exit. For the disastrous syndrome of two peoples for one country is now spreading everywhere, to the evident advantage of the strongest. In Ukraine, Pakistan, Turkey and other places. This is why it is vital that Israel and Palestine – the quintessential example of two peoples for one country – should invent a radically new, avant-garde solution to invert the equation. To unleash a movement across the region. There is yet another factor, which cannot be underestimated in a Middle East divided into religious and ethnic communities, as it has been redesigned and disfigured by the wars in Lebanon, the Gulf and Syria, and that is demographics, and with it the issue of faiths. It is true that recent work by demographers such as Emmanuel Todd, Youssef Courbage and Philippe Fargues has shown that the birth rate among Palestinians (Gaza aside) was close to that of the northern Mediterranean. Nevertheless, at the level of faith-related demography, the region into which Israel has inserted itself is not in its favour. Leaving aside the fact that the birth rate is much higher among Orthodox Jews than among secular Israelis. Hence the importance of Shlomo Sand's idea of Israeli citizenship disconnected from religion.

Although the injustice was flagrantly committed by one – Israeli – people against the – Palestinian – other, among Jewish populations there is now an understandable fear of the demographic expansion of the Muslims. To ignore this would be to reproduce – to imitate – the lying Zionist rhetoric; it would lead to a dead end. It is here that – for me – the proposals of Hazan, Sivan and Said still lack a more prosaic element that pays more attention to the source of this fear. It is only by making this fear retreat that we can enable peace to advance. It is here that ideas, however good and logical, encounter cruel limits. In 1999, Barenboim, Said and I had a discussion about the one-state solution. Although very hostile to the segregation of different communities, and aware that the Lebanese model for different faiths had failed, I wondered whether it might be necessary to invent a unique constitutional solution for a unique reality. In other words, the opposite of an ideal solution. A government that would, for example, reserve the sensitive portfolios of internal security and defence for members of the Jewish community, in order to make them feel safe in the face of Muslim demographic expansion. I accept that this is not a very cheering prospect. Writing it was merely a form of thinking aloud, trying to deal with anxieties and phobias at the root, rather than with violence and hatred on the surface. More precisely, it was a quest for reasoning that went beyond the sphere of reason alone. Ultimately, I would say that Said suggested the best solution. But the best solution in the long term is almost certainly not the best for tomorrow morning, given the current state of the region. How can we know?

An important section in *The Politics of Dispossession* provides useful shortcuts concerning both Said's relationship to Palestine and his mode of political reasoning. The latter being far more developed than it appears in certain summary overviews of his ideas. First published in *The Observer* in November 1992, 'Return to Palestine-Israel' contains his double, personal and political vision of the situation – the anger aroused in him by the physical and moral poverty and everyday erasure, city by city, of what once was Palestine, and the capacity nevertheless not to cut himself off from the Israeli reality. To imagine Israel and Palestine's paired future, despite everything, when approaching the present, where 'despite everything' reflects the extent of his universal, non-nationalist approach to the world. It was on 12 June 1992 that, for the first time since the age of twelve, he returned to his native country with his wife, Mariam, and their two children, Wadie and Najla. He writes, 'My Palestine had become a Jewish state, in which the Palestinians who stayed behind now numbered 850,000, eighteen and a half per cent of the predominantly Jewish population. The West Bank and Gaza were Occupied Territories, militarily under the control of Israeli soldiers, settlers and colonial officials. About two million Palestinians lived there.'[5] When a friend drove him to his childhood home in Talbiya, it took them nearly two hours to find it. In a supreme irony, when they reached it, the house had been transformed into an 'International Christian Embassy'.

To have found my family's house now occupied not by an Israeli Jewish family, but by a right wing Christian fundamentalist and militantly pro-Zionist group (run by a South African Boer, no less, and with a record of unsavory involvements with the Contras to boot) this was an abrupt blow for a child of Palestinian Christian parents. Anger and melancholy took me over, so that when an American woman came out of the house holding an armful of laundry and asked if she could help, all I could blurt out was an instinctive, 'no thanks.'[6]

It was not just the man, but first and foremost the child, who took the hit. The child of his parents. His return to the past can be compared to that of a patient in analysis or psychotherapy. The shock of memory reactivates the child, who had remained silent or 'unaware' at the time of the real shock. This combines with the malaise of finding the place occupied by an 'enemy' who was not the one he expected. It is no coincidence that Edward replied, 'No thanks,' rather than, 'Yes, I'd like to take a look, this is where I was born', as he would have said in different circumstances, given his natural curiosity. On the doorstep of this house, reality cast him out of time, as though into a dream. Trauma combined with a religious factor and all the guilt that goes with it. The inhabitants of the house were American militant Christians. It would have been so much simpler to knock on the door of a Jewish family, such as the Bubers, given that Martin Buber lived in that house after 1948. We have to read Edward's few lines on his return to his childhood home to gauge the extent of the appalling wound caused by the vile plot launched against him seven years later by a certain Justus Weiner. Weiner called Said a liar, a 'false prophet of Palestine' and a falsifier of history.[7] Some elements of the press relayed this accusation, saying that Edward Said was not Palestinian, his parents had never lived in Palestine, it was all lies. This sinister event, which came immediately after the Divan Orchestra began meeting in Weimar, had consequences for Said's health. His family trip to Palestine was particularly intense because it came shortly after he had received his diagnosis. The prospect of his approaching death brought a heightened sense of urgency to this trip, which took him from Jerusalem to Nazareth, Tel Aviv, Haifa and then Gaza, and to the north of the city, to the unspeakable Jabalya camp.

> The numerous children that crowd its unpaved, potholed, and chaotic little streets have a sparkle in their eyes that is totally at odds with the expression of sadness and unending suffering frozen on adult faces. There is no sewage system, the stench tears at your gut, and everywhere you look you see masses of people falling all over each other, poorly dressed, glumly making their way from one seemingly hopeless task to the other. The statistics are nightmarish.[8]

An alarming series of assessments follows. The whole is dominated by a striking lack of self-indulgence in all the stories he is told, with two recurring words: *mawt bati*, slow death. And not far away are the luxurious swimming pools of Israeli settlers, so indifferent to this human misery that they make 'Marie-Antoinette in comparison seem like an anxious radical'. The destitution described by Said is now that of several Arab peoples. Peoples who are decimated, tortured, bombed, deported. Drowned. So that the arrogance of these villas with their swimming pools, filled with the water of which the 'natives' are deprived, is, to differing degrees, an indictment of us all. The colonial impunity of Israel, its western allies and the dictatorial Arab regimes is an imposition that now taints all of us privileged people. Because the fight for Palestine, which, as Edward very clearly stated, went hand in hand with a social struggle, has failed. The bourgeoisie – which had produced people like Edward and me – has sometimes remained too closely aligned to the fight for Palestinian rights, to the detriment of other causes. In brief, we can say that the shocking proximity of swimming pools and squalor is everywhere and that, without the overthrow of capitalism in its current form, the bourgeois will go on being swimming pool users rather than denizens of squalor. This is both the advantage and disadvantage of great causes: they are so legitimate and right that they allow us to willingly spare ourselves from asking other potentially costly questions. In *The Politics of Dispossession*, which includes writings from the period 1970–94, Edward is extremely careful to adjust the principles of his fight to the evolution of the facts, over two decades. One of the most difficult issues to grasp, and understandably so, is the danger of Islamisation, which Genet, in *The Prisoner of Love*, described as that 'twilight' moment, 'an invisible transformation of the fedayeen into Shiites or members of the Muslim Brotherhood.'[9] In the early 1980s Said wrote,

> After all, the Palestinian idea in its essence opposes religious and ethnic exclusivism, which have dispossessed all four million 'non-Jews' (as Israel designates them officially), and proposes instead equality for Jews and Arabs alike. This is not an idea to be backed away from, especially at a time when Americans have been fed a diet of ideological hatred for nonwhites and for 'Islam', and when no criticism of Israel is the easiest line to take in a country that is less critical of Israeli policies than Israelis themselves.[10]

These words convey the race against time to ward off the perversion of this infernal machine. In essence, he is telling the reader, get on board with the recognition of Palestinian rights quickly, before it's too late. What do they want that is unacceptable? They want their rights and secularism. Ten years later, during his trip to Palestine-Israel, his son Wadie drew Edward's attention to the Palestinian slogans in East Jerusalem, Hebron and Nablus, some of which said 'Fateh' and others, with disturbing frequency, *Islam huwal hal* – 'Islam is the only solution'. The echoes varied. One of Edward's friends told him, 'Hamas has no visibility or recognised leadership', echoing the wishful thinking expressed to Genet by one of the Palestinian 'leaders'. Another of Edward's friends suggested that Israel and maybe Saudi Arabia were supporting Hamas. A little later he links the mistakes of the Palestinian Authority to rumours of incompetence and corruption, which were soon verified. And, in the course of a discussion with students at Birzeit University, he summed up his address to the young people as follows: 'I made, I think, one rather far-out analogy between the Israeli penchant for barbed-wire fences and the now current separation of "us" (Palestinians, Arabs, Muslims) from the West, saying that all cultures were in fact hybrid, and any attempt to push a homogenizing line was not only false but demagogic.'[11] A quarter of a century later, this warning against separation, which he repeated tirelessly until his death, has great contemporary relevance and is particularly salutary.

> The first thought that came to me after we left both Israel and Palestine was how small a role pleasure now seems to play in those two places. In Gaza, for example, swimming seems to be forbidden not by the Israelis, but by the Gazans. A harsh driven quality rules life, by necessity for Palestinians, by some other logic, which I can barely understand, for Israelis. After so many years of thinking about it, I now feel that the two peoples are locked together without much real contact or sympathy, but locked together they are, and very slowly perhaps they will improve the relationship.[12]

This piece, which Edward finished writing on 1 November 1992 – his birthday – adopts a new tone to discuss the conflict. Sickness and the threat of death were no doubt involved. This change of tone was affirmed as he prepared to meet with Daniel Barenboim.

XXII

'A man who cannot be surprised has nothing to give', wrote Arthur Schnitzler. Edward Said and Daniel Barenboim allowed themselves to be surprised by each other. From the first moment, in London, in June 1993, to the last, ten years later. Said described their meeting as a *coup de foudre*. 'Some immediate but forcefully profound recognition passed from one to the other of us, as it so fortunately but only rarely does in life.'[1] Barenboim's musical genius, extreme mental clarity, empathy and responsiveness, despite his frantic round of concerts, led Edward to write, 'This friendship transformed my life.'[2] The word 'life' returns in these two phrases as it did every time Edward spoke of Barenboim. As life and movement are almost synonymous, we can gauge what this relationship brought him at the emotional, musical, political and intellectual levels. In addition to their obvious affinities, the two men shared a vision of 'the enemy' that was neither phobic nor reductive. For both, 'the enemy' did not have a single image, set of features and form. It was this spontaneous agreement that enabled them to take a major step that carried them beyond what they knew, to show them what they could not see, or could see only partly. Without compromising their beliefs. But making them more permeable, less likely to become fixed in exclusive certainties. Freed from rivalry, their friendship created between them something that was normally denied – the path that leads from intelligence to curiosity about the other, to recognition. Without fear of disagreement, without stopping movement. One reason why the path became so quickly and firmly apparent was that, before trying to understand each other, they listened. Crucially, they enjoyed the process. They met on common ground brought to life by the energy they employed to make it exist and keep it going. As in music. 'Music is not about being but about becoming', Barenboim said to Said in a conversation recorded in Weimar in 1999.[3] 'We are ever becoming – never being', wrote Conrad to his friend Garnett a century earlier, noted by Said in his first book.[4] Barenboim and Said were clearly on the same wavelength from the outset. They didn't always say the same things, but they spoke the same language. A language that wants meaning to owe its existence to what comes before and after it, like a musical note. In their modes of argument, there was a zone that they fully shared – an awareness of the provisional and paradoxical that opened the way to humour, flexibility and that most fertile of margins for manoeuvre, the postponement of conflict. It was a pleasure to see them talk, to imagine them (Edward often referred to Barenboim in his letters), to see at work the natural, effortless effort of two wills that had decided to contradict each other only in the service of a new starting point, on condition of continuity. They wanted the same thing: equality. I couldn't say which of them went further down the path. I don't think the question arose in those terms. Their desire, their joy at meeting, knowing each other, simply released them from the reflexes of political disagreement. Barenboim understood from the first that the asymmetry of power relations between Israel and Palestine obliged him to recognise that there was more than one step to be taken, at the political level, to make the meeting work. He took those steps. He recognised the brutality done to the Palestinians by the Israeli authorities, the chain of injustices and humiliations inflicted. In an interview given shortly after Said's death, Barenboim said, 'Israeli governments are persecuting a minority, in disregard for the entire history of Judaism and all the ethics of Judaism, we who were a minority for two thousand years are now oppressing another people, another minority. It's time to realise this.'[5]

Barenboim heard Edward's anger and, in doing so, soothed it. He orchestrated their differences in such a way as to create a whole within which there was room for each. Their meeting illustrated Césaire's words, often cited by Edward: 'No race has the monopoly of beauty, intelligence or strength, and victory makes room for all.'[6] As in music, Barenboim moved away from literal readings and did not cling to presuppositions. In a series of dialogues recorded in their book *Parallels and Paradoxes*, Barenboim told Said 'if you try to objectively reproduce what is printed and nothing more, not only is this not possible to do – and, therefore, there's no fidelity – it is also a complete act of cowardice because it means that you haven't gone to the trouble to understand the interrelations and what the dosage is, to speak of nothing else.'[7] The essence of his point is that, in this separation, music has no chance of existing. Edward then intervenes to include tempo. Daniel agrees, while observing that some musicians commit 'the fatal mistake of first deciding on the tempo. They take a metronome, sometimes given by the composer, which is inevitably too fast because when the composer writes the metronome marking, he doesn't have the weight of sound. He only has the imagination in his brain.'[8] Thus, Boulez came to amend the metronome tempo of his score for *Notations VII*, which was originally far faster than when conducted by Barenboim. 'How did that happen?' asked Barenboim, to which Boulez replied, 'Simple. When I compose I cook with water, when I conduct I cook with fire.' At this stage of the dialogue, about halfway through the book, Barenboim attempts a comparison with politics. 'No matter what you think of the Oslo Accord – in other words, it had a chance or it didn't have a chance – it lost all chance of succeeding when the tempo, the speed at which it was proceeding, became so slow.' Edward chooses not to interrupt him. However, he thought, as he repeatedly said, that the process was dead before it got going. He didn't discuss the issue of the settlements, their eviction and prohibition, nor did he refer to the dispossession and injustice done to the Palestinians. In his view – which I share – the Oslo Accord was stillborn. Barenboim pursues his direction of thought and moves away from the issue of the Oslo Accords to something else that is too often forgotten, the *legato*. 'I mean, *legato* is also a question of fidelity to the text. In other words, we have become so obsessed with this machine of tempo that the content is becoming absolutely separated. And therefore, it is also a victim of this mania that we have towards specialization, in the sense of dissecting elements and making them independent.' Edward can only agree with this warning, which coincides with his critique of 'experts', compartmentalised knowledge and, when extended to politics, the divisive readings that give rise to xenophobia. This is how their dialogue survived disagreement. They didn't deny it, but they abstained from giving it a central place. As there were only two of them, they could defy the conventions of the endless dialogue between the Arabs and Israelis. They avoided sentimentality and words that had lost their meaning. Instead of listing their grievances and the reasons why they were right, they made a connection – connections. They went straight to the heart of a common problem. What can we do to understand each other when we have the means? Peace broke out between these two men, naturally, all by itself. And this understanding, which was more human than political, gave birth to a project, a unique orchestra.[9] In reality, Said and Barenboim approached peace from its starting point – the retreat of fear. They invented a 'beginning' that side-stepped the infernal, dead-end logic of chronology. They agreed on a set of references that enabled them to understand each other without reviewing their disagreements one by one. Basically, they declared the start of something that was undoubtedly not a political solution, but proof of the limits that can be imposed on war by the desire for peace. I wonder whether this rare friendship was not also, above and beyond itself, a model for a different understanding of what, for half a century, has been wrongly termed 'Arab–Israeli dialogue'. If I had to sum up their fundamental difference, above and beyond their respective connections to Israel and Palestine, I would say that Said proceeded as a historian and musicologist, on the basis of an ethical and moral corpus, Barenboim as a musician, on the basis of neutral ground that made it possible to accept morality before the point where it became a limit or end of non-acceptance. One had a mission, the other a vocation, in the sense that Edward returned more often to reality, while Daniel exchanged it with another reality. This is one difference between the intellectual and the artist. So, on the question of fidelity to the text, Said intervenes to reduce the distance from the original text advocated by Barenboim: 'The work that editors do, in collating manuscripts, in collating notebooks, or at least giving them a presence so that the interpreter or the reader can return to them, is crucial.'[10] Then he tempers his words by adding, 'There's no such thing as faithfully reproducing a text . . . I think there's a kind of interplay constantly between the individuality of the reader, performer, interpreter . . . and the whole history of decisions, consensus, and transmission of a text from its history, whether it was five minutes ago or two hundred years ago, that makes it available in the present.'[11] These samples of their dialogue give an idea of its flexibility. Quite the opposite of what happened at the political level between those in power. Barenboim opened up a field of possibility by breaking with the context of Israeli bad faith, the lie organised supposedly in the service of security. Edward did the same, by stepping away from persecution and a truth closed to anything that might lead the cursor to be moved. How? By anticipating rather than reacting. The great difference between the two men resided in the fact that one, Barenboim, was working in the universal language of music, while the other used a critical language, applied in a way that enabled its universal potential to emerge. One is Jewish, Argentinian, Israeli, and German and, in 2008, he became Palestinian. He is a citizen of the world. He is the opposite of a victim and he knows it. Edward, born Protestant, has two conflicting identities: he is Palestinian and American. He has a cause to promote and he is, from every point of view, more invested in and pinned down by reality. Daniel is unencumbered. The elements that constitute him accumulate but do not fight. When a problem arises that has no solution, he turns his back. His duality is not conflictual, unlike Edward's and mine. His double – for he does have one – is not hostile to him. Barenboim is double in the sense that he is twice himself. Without guilt. And without fear. At least that is how I see him. He is seconded, yes, that's the word. I have rarely seen anyone so well seconded by himself.

Said wrote,

> In August 1999, [Daniel,] Yo-Yo Ma, and I convened a carefully selected group of seventy-eight Arab and Israeli musicians aged eighteen to twenty-five in Weimar, that year's European cultural capital . . . For three weeks there were master classes with Daniel and Yo-Yo, plus first desk players from Chicago and Berlin, plus chamber music, plus seven hours of daily orchestra rehearsals, plus evening discussions led by the two of us. No days off. About three afternoons a week, Barenboim drove off to conduct (by memory naturally) *Tristan* and *Meistersinger* at Bayreuth, then would return at 2:00 in the morning ready to start rehearsals at 9:30. By the end, after rivetingly intense, humorous, profoundly instructive and inventive measure-by-measure drills without a score anywhere near him, Daniel's orchestra emerged, tackling the Schumann Cello Concerto with a superb Yo-Yo, the Beethoven Seventh, Mozart's Two Piano Concerto (an Israeli and Palestinian pianist as elegant soloists), and even an overture for the final concert, played to a sold out spell-bound audience in Weimar's main hall.[12]

I had the good fortune to be present for this orchestra's beginnings in that extraordinary August. To see groups that had spontaneously separated, Arabs on one side, Israelis on the other, gradually draw closer until they merged. To see animosity give way to desire, perhaps even love, between an Israeli cellist and Syrian violinist. To see trust form through the workshops Said ran with the Israeli musicians and Barenboim with the Arab musicians. Both men abandoned the notion of identity, of a camp. The day Edward decided to go to Buchenwald, with no obligation placed on those who did not want to, all, or almost, went with him. On the wooded path leading to the camp, one of the Israeli violinists went up to him and whispered in his ear. His father had been imprisoned in Buchenwald, and had only just escaped death there. Daniel didn't know this. It was Edward who told him. Once at the site, the person who broke down was not the Israeli violinist, but the Egyptian cellist. At the door to the crematorium his teeth started chattering and he began to tremble all over, saying, 'I don't know what's wrong with me, I'm dying of cold'. We covered him with our jackets. Unlike him, his Israeli comrades knew what they had come to see. I was struck by the sight of artificial flowers in the crematorium. As the decoration of horror, it was beyond bad taste. I was reminded of it in Weimar two days later, at an exhibition of Hitler's daubs with Edward. Visiting Goethe's house, walking in the footsteps of Bach, listening to Wagner conducted by Barenboim in Bayreuth, with the orchestra in the pit, our bodies still and straight on seats that did not permit the slightest slump, made those days in Germany among the most unforgettable of my life. Life, in tandem, as Said wrote, with Barenboim's 'seemingly infinite capacity for taking the material of music and giving it the density and complexity of life itself, life elaborating itself into pattern, structure, order, energy and, not least, surprise and joy.'[13] Since that time, the Divan Orchestra has constantly toured the world. It has also led to another project, the Barenboim-Said Academy. Opened in 2016, this school offers ninety students from the Middle East the opportunity to study with Barenboim and other top-flight musicians and composers. 'Barenboim, the artistic director of the Staatsoper next door, said that, just as with the orchestra, the academy was inspired by conversations he had had with his friend, the late American-Palestinian professor of literature Edward Said.'[14] He calls it an 'experiment in utopia'. Strike

imaginations. This was Nelson Mandela's advice to Said in relation to Palestine. His advice was followed.

When Said published *Musical Elaborations*, he had yet to meet
Barenboim. His approach to musical interpretation was linked to
his ideas on literary criticism. He writes notably, 'What interests
me is the way the best interpreters of poetry and music allow both
their audience and themselves (self-conviction being not the least
of the interpreter's virtues) the proposition that the work being
presented is as if created by the performer.'[15] The shift he imperceptibly makes between musical and literary interpretation
elicited a reaction from Barenboim, who insists that there is a
difference in status between sounds and words. 'The element of
sound is very different, in other words when you talk about music,
you're not talking about interpretation in the same way that you
would talk about the text at all.'[16] He suggests that we might link
the reading of a score to that of a poem, but playing a score

> involves a physical act that requires the musician to have under-
> standing and knowledge of the physical side of music, which
> has to do with acoustics, which has to do with overtone,
> which has to do with harmonic relationship . . . And this is
> why I believe that the word 'interpretation' was misused and
> understood by many people . . . You have to understand, first
> of all, the physicality of how the sound of Beethoven's Fifth
> really operates; and how the orchestra has to be balanced; and
> how the texture has to be sometimes thick and sometimes thin;
> what is the speed of the dynamics – in other words, it says
> *crescendo*; the *crescendo* mark is written vertically through the
> whole score, but if all the instruments of the orchestra start
> to *crescendo* at the same time, you don't hear everything.
> Obviously, the horns, trumpets, and timpani will cover the rest
> of the orchestra. Therefore, this concept of fidelity to the text
> in music is much more relative, and relative in the sense not
> that you're not bound by a contract, as you say, but more rela-
> tive in the sense that you sin by omission.[17]

At this point Edward rearranges the comparison, saying,

> I wonder whether the interesting parallel might be not from
> literature to music but from music to literature in the interpre-
> tation of a text. In other words, whether one could base oneself
> on some of the things that you've just said and apply them to
> the reading of a poem. For instance, you take a poetic line of
> Keats: 'Thou still unravish'd bride of quietness' . . . It's not just
> a matter of saying, 'Well now, of course I understand what a
> bride is; I understand what quiet is; and I understand what
> unravish'd means; therefore, I understand the line.' It doesn't
> work that way because the poetic object is a whole series of rela-
> tionships, internal to the poem, which you need to understand
> before you can, if you will, 'read' it.

He goes on, 'But then, there's also the question of what would
then be the equivalent of the realization of sound . . . the physical
quality of the relationship to sound. In that respect music is
unique, quite on its own.'[18] Barenboim sums it up differently:

> If you really are able to build a phrase with a continuous
> sound, so that each note follows the preceding note – starts at
> the level that the preceding note ended and finishes the note
> at the level that the next note starts – you already have, through
> this element of sound, an element of tension and an element of
> something keeping you in mid-air, because otherwise it would
> drop the sound, which means it would drop to the floor. And
> therefore, without any dynamic, before you even start with all
> that, there is an element of tension in sound that you simply
> don't have in words.[19]

This physical investment involved in musical interpretation was
familiar to Said. He had experienced it from a very early age when
playing the piano. And he was desperately striving to combine
sound and word in a synthesis. This quest perhaps reflected an

intellectual's adieu to the musician he could have been. I also see here the mark of his unique style, in which words lived intensely and equally in all the forms in which he used them, written or spoken, thought or silent. Nietzsche described the word as 'a nervous excitation'. And in a letter to Wells, Conrad confided, 'For me, writing – *the only possible writing* – is just simply the conversion of nervous force into phrases.'[20] This nervousness metabolised by thought, dressed in meaning through the association of words, reminds me of a void filling with physical energy that, without being comparable, is not unrelated to the energy Barenboim talks about. Of course, the fundamental difference remains. But let us say that Edward got as close as possible to the zones common to music and thought, where meaning always risks becoming lost and falling to the ground. It was not for nothing that Adorno occupied such a key place in his work. The German musicologist also hesitated between a musical and an intellectual career. A composer and pianist, he gave up the idea of playing for a living, in exchange for thought of an extremely sophisticated kind, elitist sometimes to the point of hermeticism.

In the end it is Adorno's unmatched technicality that is so significant. His analyses of Schoenberg's method in *The Philosophy of New Music* give words and concepts to the inner workings of a formidably complex new outlook in another medium, and he does so with a prodigiously exact technical awareness of both mediums, words and tones.[21]

This quotation well expresses the reasons for Said's fascination with the author of *Negative Dialectics*. He reconciled – or at least brought together in thought – the destiny of words and sounds. The element of functioning that they share. Not only that, he made possible a simultaneous understanding of music and politics, notably developing a link between the cultural industry and the coming to power of Nazi barbarism, between consumerism and its threat to art. Since 'works of art' are in their essence 'ascetic and unashamed' where the 'cultural industry' is 'pornographic and prudish'.[22] Adorno gave Said an irreplaceable network of associations, drawing on disciplines that are usually isolated from each other. Cerebrally, Adorno offered him what Conrad gave him psychologically: the space that best suited his obsessions and inner divisions. For example, the possibility of thinking about imperialist and/or capitalist history at the same time as the history of music, and drawing on the writing of music itself. With the movement from Beethoven to Schoenberg as a historical tipping point, Beethoven defying synthesis in his late works, Schoenberg imposing intransigence from his beginnings. When Said talks to Barenboim about Adorno, a polite silence seems to hover in the air. In reality, Adorno's intellectualism was a long, long way from the methods of Barenboim, who seeks neither proof nor conclusions. He is all about movement; he seeks without pause, without tearing himself apart. When, in the spirit of Adorno, Said suggests there is a dividing line between, on the one hand, classical music and music redesigned as a mass phenomenon (rock, hip-hop, etc.), and, on the other, music that is less and less accessible to the majority, Barenboim disagrees somewhat, then changes the subject. 'An artist, to be true to himself, has to have the courage to be totally uncompromising; and the politician, to be true to himself, has to have the art of compromising at the tip of his fingers; otherwise he's not a politician. And therefore to be an artist in a political society is to go against the mainstream.'[23] It is notable that Barenboim separates without dividing. The 'artist' has his logic, and so does the 'politician'. Unlike Edward, he avoids confrontation. What both share is their participation in history, in collective life. In continuity.

'How is it possible that something [music] that can teach you so much about the world, nature, the universe, and, for more religious people, God – that something that is so clearly able to teach you so many things can serve as a means of escape from precisely those things?'[24] By 'escape' Barenboim means the immoral use that can be made of music. From physical to metaphysical, from beauty to immorality, the two men suddenly find themselves taken onto the terrain of God. Barenboim sidesteps: 'I don't think you can speak about music. You can only speak of a subjective reaction to it.'[25] Finding himself on shifting ground, Edward mentions mysticism, 'the ineffable, the unspoken, the unreachable'[26] – unaccustomed vocabulary for him – then returns to two familiar staples of his musical culture: 'One thinks of Messiaen and certainly of Bach – there's an attempt not so much to approach the divine but to embody the divine.' He goes on,

> It's quite strange, for me anyway, being somebody who is totally not religious. I'm quite secular in that respect. But I'm very drawn to works of that sort, and not only because of the religious element. It's because I keep thinking, in the case of Bach, whose forms are so rationalistic in a way, that the representation of the biblical drama in a staggeringly rich and compelling work like the *Saint Matthew Passion* can be explained by saying, 'Well, there must be some actual rational law that explains it'. But the work always seems to be moving away from you. I think that's the fascination. Not that you say, 'Well, we're only approaching it', you actually feel you're getting closer to it, but it's always drawing away.[27]

Edward's expectation – 'there must be a law' – makes me think of Proust writing about *In Search of Lost Time* – 'Where I was seeking great laws, they said I was digging through details', and also, 'I had the misfortune to start a book with the word "I" and it was immediately assumed that rather than trying to discover general laws I was "analysing myself" in the individual, detestable sense of the word.'[28] Like Proust, Said was seeking the keys to the mystery of man in man. For both of them, music was the site of the transference or projection of what man knows, onto what he does not know and, conversely, the quintessential site of the dissolution and reconstitution of time. It is Vinteuil's sonata that gives Swann the means to succeed, where his love for Odette has failed:

to access the continuity of the past and preserve his secret intact –
he need only listen to this music to find it again – whatever the
damage caused by age, disillusionment and forgetting. It is this
magic that Proust refers to when he says that a particular name
mentioned in a book 'contains among its syllables the strong wind
and bright sunlight of the day when we were reading it.'[29] When
thought falls prey to memory, itself prey to a state of dozing or
dreaming (which unfolds beyond time by definition), it is true
that it works in a similar way to music. Close to, but without,
music. As small black signs on a white surface, words and notes
both act as levers for a world that takes on independent life. In the
case of words, silence can seep in anywhere, any time, without
destroying the edifice. In the case of music, silence is at either end,
before and after. If it enters into the unfolding of the notes, it kills
them, it stops the music. Unless it is written into the score, in the
way that notes are, in other words as a pause within the sound,
which itself rests on a great silence. Said takes up Adorno's
observation that 'late Beethoven is really the presagement of
the alienated music of Schoenberg', and asks, 'What are some of the
characteristics of late Beethoven? Well, late Beethoven defies
synthesis. Some of the pieces, like the last sonata, are unfinished;
it's only two movements.' 'And there's also an element of constant
interruption', adds Barenboim. This state of being unfinished
feeds a discomfort that destabilises the earlier bourgeois order. It
is a door open to questions without answers – more precisely, to
the lack of an answer. And so to anxiety. 'Why does Wagner mark
such a critical juncture in music? Why is there always the question
of what happened after Wagner? There's one overriding answer:
the loss of a tonality. With the loss of tonality, there is the loss of a
certain dimension of music, which is not possible without
harmony.'[30] This rupture can undoubtedly be linked to painting
and literature; Wagner died around the time that Joyce and Picasso
were born, Schoenberg had been born a little earlier. The work of
these artists deals with the same challenge, the same upheaval: the
end of time with borders, contained by time. Its permeability and

tearing. The triumph of moment over duration. The infiltration of form by dissonance. The end of 'defined functions'. The beginning of deconstruction. And, with this undermining of benchmarks, the need to resist the threat of chaos it engendered and to invent new rigours. Baudelaire's beauty, that 'dream of stone' reigning in the blue like a 'misunderstood Sphinx', was cracking. However much it hated 'the movement which displaces lines', it was exposed to them.[31] Obsessed with the question of beginnings and ends, Said placed himself at the cusp of these two times, one sanctified, under the guardianship of a single God, the other profane, open to the pantheon of disagreement. In the second, the singing voice is close to the speaking voice. The friction between them gives rise to a third voice, one that, according to Adorno, gave music autonomy from society. Said says the same thing in a different way in 'From Silence to Sound and Back Again':

> To overcome silence, to extend musical expression beyond the final cadence, Beethoven opened up the realm of language whose capacity for explicit human utterance says more on its own than music can. Hence to Wagner the tremendous significance of the eruption of voice and word into the instrumental texture of the Ninth Symphony. What he saw there was a humanized embodiment of language defying the silence of finality and of music itself.[32]

Here again, Said's signposts and anchor points are pieces of a puzzle that simultaneously write his self-portrait beneath the layers of analysis. So, his book *On Late Style* does not deal solely with late style, but, through it, the 'counter-current' contained in the subtitle: *Music and Literature Against the Grain*. This counter-current precisely reflects the movement of Edward's life and work. Which from the beginning gave him the feeling of being 'not quite right'. For his words from the end of *On Late Style* on Beethoven's relationship to time – at once anticipatory and retrospective – apply equally well to his own. 'The masterpieces of

Beethoven's final decade are late to the extent that they are beyond
their own time, ahead of it in terms of daring and startling
newness, later than it in that they describe a return or home-
coming to realms forgotten or left behind by the relentless forward
march of history.'[33] This back and forth, from the time to come to
time past, perfectly describes Said's intellectual trajectory. What
is it that characterises his back and forth? His sense of time passing or the strength of the link between time that precedes and
time that follows, the more or less conscious fear of seeing the link
broken by one interrogation too many, the speed with which he
gathers issues and moves them forward together, like musical
instruments guided by his baton. Hence his great talent for improv-
isation. Hence also the uneasy question he put to Barenboim, who
had observed 'every great work of art has two faces: one is toward
its own time and one toward eternity.' Some music, he says, is
timeless. 'Why call it timeless?' Edward objects. 'You're in time,
you're not out of time.' 'Timeless in the sense that it is not only
limited to that time. It is permanently contemporary,' Daniel
replies. If Edward found it easier to deal with the absence of
place – being 'out of place' – than the absence of time – being 'out
of time' – it is because human history and chronology were his
vital reference points in facing the loss of spaces and territory. For
him, this temporal challenge was overlaid by a geographical back
and forth – from East to West, from Said to Edward – that is
illustrated even in the graphic aspect of his handwriting. Every
letter is ruled at once by the gallop and the lasso, the open sea and
the return to port. The discipline, sometimes even the repressed
nature of his writing, was accompanied by a constant nervousness,
a physical tension reflecting the need to hold firm in two places,
two times. The present was for him the time of provisional synthesis between past and future. The limited time of recapitulation.
That's life. Life to be made again as soon as it has been made. The
before and the after, each enriched, each threatened by the other.
In the best case, unified, unbothered by borders, conducted like
an orchestra – then it's music. The historical transition from

Beethoven to Wagner, which Said describes in the last part of *Musical Elaborations*, reappears towards the end of his conversations with Barenboim. For the latter, 'there was a musical language and a kind of rational consensus that existed for generations from Bach until Wagner, then it's no longer there. It's as if it went out of existence.'[34] For Said, citing Adorno, the beauty of modern music, inaugurated by Schoenberg, lies in its challenge to beauty. He says to Barenboim,

> I'm just wondering how far one can take the Adornian argument: that the significance of music is that, by the very fact of its bristly complexity, it is an indictment of the inhumanity of a society that forces it to play the role of the great opposite of the society – a society that is all about consumerism and commodification, on the one hand, and about inhumanity, on the other. The inheritors of Schoenberg would have to be caught in this dialectic.[35]

The musical moment that breaks the silence before itself being broken by silence is, in reality, a kind of absolute moment that provisionally contains all time. And if, for example, this moment is the second movement of Beethoven's Fifth Piano Concerto, mentioned by Barenboim, it is, he says, a moment of serenity and harmony that others would call God. On the other hand, if we listen to Beethoven's last works, we are struck by the fact that, in the words of Maynard Solomon, their 'aggressive, dotted-rhythmic polyphonic textures [create] a simultaneous sense of irresistible motion and unbearable strain.'[36] At the intersection of the two, Beethoven explores the links between beauty and horror. Or, more precisely, their compatibility. How is it, indeed, that classical music can be so greatly appreciated by a torturer? Such a thing would be impossible in the realm of words. This autism of music is, in a way – let us return to the example of the *St Matthew Passion* – the most sublime form of beauty. Bergman gives it a remarkable place in *Saraband*, one of his last films. When the old man, Johan, full of both hatred and humanity, shuts himself away in his room with Bruckner's Ninth Symphony, though his beloved granddaughter Karin beats on his door and calls for help, he doesn't hear her, he hears nothing, only music. Neither love nor hate nor fear can break down these impenetrable walls of sound. Music is all-powerful. Time out of time. 'For the beautiful', said Rilke, 'is nothing but the onset of that terror we can scarcely endure, and we are fascinated because it calmly disdains to obliterate us.'[37]

When Barenboim mentions the use of Beethoven's music by the Nazis, he states,

The moment a composer like Beethoven has actually finished writing a piece, that piece becomes independent of him. It becomes part of the world. The qualities that he has put in don't necessarily stay there. So, they can be interpreted or misinterpreted, used or abused, as we have seen in the different political trends too. But I believe there is an intrinsic moral. Why? Because I believe that the struggle is an essential, integral part of the expression in Beethoven's music. If you don't feel the struggle to get the intensity of the sound – if you're able to produce the sound in a light-hearted, athletic way – it cannot have the intensity. And this applies as much to the soft playing, to the *dolce espressivo* of Beethoven, or the slow movement in the Fourth Symphony, for instance – as it does to the heroic gestures of the Fifth Symphony or the *Eroica*; this element of struggle, Beethoven was really the first composer who used the effect of a very long *crescendo* and then a *subito piano*, a drop in the dynamic. It requires a lot of courage and energy to really go with the *crescendo* to the end, as if you're getting to the precipice and then stop short. The easy way out is, toward the end, to let the energy go. And the same thing when it goes from the *crescendo* into a big *fortissimo*. This is the most difficult thing – to have control of the *crescendo*, the gradual build-up, so that there is enough left for the end.[38]

Having established that music is neither moral nor immoral, but amoral, Barenboim again insists on the investment required of the one who plays it: 'It's not ethical to make a *crescendo* only with your brain, your whole body has to be involved in that.'[39] And to reach the height of intensity, he advocates an association that is not self-evident: that of awe and courage. 'You get a sense of awe, which is passive and, on the other side, the courage to do, which is active.'[40] It is very likely that Edward found in this division of energies – passive, active, transgressive and awed – the exact portrait of the musician as he understood him.

This digression reminds me of a meeting a few years ago in Istanbul. The pianist Murray Perahia had come to give a concert, at the end of which I and other friends had been invited to dinner by the conductor Cem Mansur and his wife, the actress Lale, at their house in Arnavutköy. There were some Turkish musicians there, and also the widow of the conductor Georg Solti. Perahia was sitting in the middle of a sofa, flanked to his right and left by the twin pianists Güher and Süher Pekinel and talking to them quietly. Until the moment when, as is my irritating habit, I joined the conversation and derailed it. 'How can you explain', I asked Perahia, 'that this kind of beauty could move a Nazi leader to tears?' The discussion continued on this insoluble theme until Madame Solti, a stately woman and great music lover with a very choice vocabulary, came into the room and asked what we were talking about. 'Oh!' she sighed, before shouting – standing there in the middle of the room – 'Music can be a horror! Music can be a horror!' I can still hear it. If she'd said, 'Beauty can be a horror,' it would have been the same. It seems to me that Edward's obsession, in music as in literature, is not unrelated to this spectre of horror lurking behind beauty. Is it any coincidence that Kurtz's last words in *Heart of Darkness*, cited by Edward on countless occasions, are 'The horror, the horror'? 'What exactly did he mean?' he asked me several times, and every time as if it were the first. His beginning of an answer, in his thesis on Conrad, was as follows: 'The horror of it all is that his soul cannot finally maintain both light and darkness, although he requires both.'[41] In Freudian terms, his ego, rather than his soul, is pulled in different directions by two extreme drives that destroy him. This interpretation perhaps says more about Said's anxiety than that of Kurtz. I mean that, for Said and like Nostromo, Kurtz embodies the danger he was always fighting against. The danger of seeing his duality degenerate into a force of destruction and his elevated sense of morality give way, under the pressure of what Thomas Mann called 'the silent Satanism'.[42]

When, a year after Kurtz's death, Conrad through his character Marlow takes on the unspeakable pain of Kurtz's fiancée, who 'carried her sorrowful head as though she were proud of that sorrow, as though she would say, I – I alone know how to mourn for him as he deserves', he sees her as 'one of those creatures that are not the playthings of time. For her he had died only yesterday.'[43] Her love had the same power as music to abolish time. A moment before, Marlow has remembered how Kurtz cast a shadow darker than night, 'his abject pleading, his abject threats, the colossal scale of his vile desires, the meanness, the torment, the tempestuous anguish of his soul.'[44] Who, ultimately, was Kurtz? Who was this ivory trader sent to Africa by a Belgian company, this charismatic, gifted man whose principles had been swallowed up by boundless greed? 'His mother was half-English, his father half-French. All Europe contributed to the making of Kurtz.'[45] Gifted with unlimited powers of eloquence, reigning like a demi-god over the jungle peoples, he is described as a prophet by the chief of Inner Station. '"He is a prodigy," he said at last. "He is an emissary of pity, and science, and progress, and devil knows what else. We want," he began to declaim suddenly, "for the guidance of the cause intrusted to us by Europe, so to speak, higher intelligence, wide sympathies, a singleness of purpose."'[46] A third of the way through the narrative, taking shape behind the magnified portrait of this man, we see the scale of the crimes and sordid lies that have made him. For Conrad, as for Marlow, lies are horror. 'You know I hate, detest, and can't bear a lie, not because I am straighter than the rest of us, but simply because it appals me.

There is a taint of death, a flavour of mortality in lies – which is exactly what I hate and detest in the world – what I want to forget.'[47] Edward would undoubtedly have preferred to say, 'What I want to fight,' rather than to forget. A little later Marlow goes on, 'I became in an instant as much of a pretence as the rest of the bewitched pilgrims.'[48] However ironic and lucid he may be, Marlow is no fool, he is aware of the danger, aware of that element of Kurtz that he carries within himself.

> A voice. He was very little more than a voice. And I heard – him – it – this voice – other voices – all of them were so little more than voices – and the memory of that time itself lingers around me, impalpable, like a dying vibration of one immense jabber, silly, atrocious, sordid, savage, or simply mean, without any kind of sense. Voices, voices – even the girl herself – now.[49]

Yes, the girl, as much in love now as on the first day, credulous, dressed in black, 'this fair hair, this pale visage, this pure brow',[50] this certainty – 'no one knew him so well as I' – her faith – '"Who was not his friend who had heard him speak once?" she was saying. "He drew men towards him by what was best in them . . . It is the gift of the great."'[51] On the one hand, Marlow has to deal with the blind fidelity of this great love – Conrad believes in it so little – and, on the other, the truth about the imperialist tyrant and killer of black people. He is prey to a feeling he is totally unused to, and Conrad also – 'infinite pity'. The girl begs him to tell her the last words of this man, Kurtz, who died in her absence. '"I think of his loneliness. Nobody near to understand him as I would have understood. Perhaps no one to hear . . ." "To the very end," says Marlow, shakily. "I heard his very last words . . ." "Repeat them," she murmured in a heart-broken tone. "I want – I want – something – something – to – to live with."' Marlow says,

> I was on the point of crying at her, 'Don't you hear them?' The dusk was repeating them in a persistent whisper all around us,

in a whisper that seemed to swell menacingly like the first whisper of a rising wind. 'The horror! The horror!' 'His last word – to live with,' she insisted. 'Don't you understand I loved him – I loved him – I loved him!' I pulled myself together and spoke slowly. 'The last word he pronounced was – your name.'

Horror is temporarily returned to silence. 'The tranquil waterway . . . seemed to lead into the heart of an immense darkness.'[52] In the language of Beethoven, the way led from his early sonatas to his late quartets. In Schoenberg's, the way led to the heart of the forest: *Erwartung*, the opera with one act, one voice, or the anxious waiting of a woman in love about to discover her crime. In the language of Freud, the way led to the heart of the id. Marlow chose to save the young woman in love from the truth. What would Edward have done in his place? Perhaps he would have said nothing, I don't know.

XXIII

You died just now. It was ten years ago. Our time, in the meantime, hasn't stopped. Sometimes it's as flat as a lake, I can run over it, helter-skelter, without damaging it. Sometimes I work miracles: I create a wave of the surface. An unbreachable hour that stands alone, like music, that the hours on either side cannot touch. We are wrong to give the name memory to this overturning of the present by the past, which is an event far superior to the two separated times. I don't remember you, I relive you, the same and differently. When it's the same, the image comes alive on a pinpoint, then dies. When it's different, it's easier to live with.

I have written to you a lot. Almost as much as when you were alive. The words erased themselves. We were too strong for me alone.

I can only manage to write to you a little when I give up trying.

After rereading these notes written five years ago, I wonder, now, why the last scene of *Heart of Darkness* came back here in this form. Why in the context of music? What did we have in common, you and I, with Kurtz and the young woman in love? The fall of Kurtz embodies all that you fought against. And she, credulous, naive, the total opposite of the lucidity that I have always practised to the point of fanaticism. To the point, often, of hurting us cruelly, you and me. And yet there is something of us in them. What? The awareness we each had of being at the mercy of a miserable double? 'At the mercy' is not the right phrase. We loved each other too much to be 'at the mercy of'. Let us say that we knew we were under threat. And that this threat rendered us all the more jealously protective of us. Certain of living a love that was far greater than our attacks, far stronger than the blows we struck against it. And we were not wrong. I am your posthumous proof, living proof of a love that was attained, in the face of threats. We went as far as possible in loving each other with two loves, one passionate, the other tender. You had a sometimes naive obsession with truth. Like that young woman? And I had a morbid penchant for truth. Like Kurtz? Like her, I waited feverishly to know what your last words were. The words that our friend told me helped me go on living. Were there others that said the opposite? Perhaps. I even have a memory, if I force myself not to push it aside, of some-one else, not so close, who gave me to understand that you were very angry with me at the end of your life. The year we had stopped seeing each other. I stopped her by saying, 'When Edward was angry he was capable of denying the thing he cared about most. He was capable of betrayal.' I whispered that she was wrong to think I had been deceived. And I was right about that, Edward, you were capable of betrayal. You betrayed, above all because betrayal was what you feared most. You betrayed when you were losing whatever protected you against the betrayal of others. Alone, you were too much alone to bear it. With me it was some-thing else. I didn't betray, I destroyed. I slammed the door. It was my way of being faithful to us. Of not betraying what had happened between us. Of not prolonging it in a half-life. But isn't destroying another way of betraying? It is. So, I betrayed too. We both betrayed the extraordinary couple I watch walking hand in hand, the two hands as one with ten fingers, deep in the pocket of your green Loden coat. And that couple, that inextinguishable you and me, that beauty, worth all the sufferings it asked of us, will always elude me, no matter how hard I have tried to give it life in this book, as the meaning of music eludes us. And what if a love like ours was too fine a conquest for me to settle for what's left when one end is lost? I have loved you too much to accept loving you less or differently. You too, in a way. You are certainly not Kurtz, and nor am I. Neither of us are the young woman who loves him. But there is something of both of them in our two shadows, there is the terrifying fear of having lost what we won. That we were so proud of. The horror of having seen our love 'touched' by a sickness it had scorned. Last night, rereading pages of *Doctor Faustus*, I thought, 'Where Nostromo and Kurtz, ravaged by greed, ultimately sacrifice their ideas, starting with love, Adrian begins by sacrificing love to the ideal of knowledge and creation.' In all three cases, it is love that is sacrificed. And the ideal is a killer. We didn't sacrifice love, but we did experience the terrible foretaste of losing it. In New York in 2000, I wrote, 'My nerves are giving me the ravages of madness without madness. I have become a heroic monster.' We were no longer managing to keep things together. You were devoured by illness, while a dentist's surgical error had led to a constant burning sensation in my mouth. We were swimming against a tide, no longer knowing where it would end. In the same period, you were writing the essays of *On Late Style*. The one that looks at Thomas Mann, through *Death in Venice*, concludes with Britten, and Adorno's words on the musician, with which the book ends: 'Subjective and objective. Objective is the fractured landscape, subjective the light in which – alone – it glows into life. He [the artist] does not bring about their harmonious synthesis. As the power of dissociation, he tears them apart in time, in order, perhaps, to preserve them for the eternal. In the history of art late works are the catastrophes.'[1] The late works of our love followed the movement of those you describe in your last pages. The movement in which the past, seen as without a future, ultimately requires irony to undo the illusory and patient constructions of time, just before death. Who knows, my Edward, perhaps our 'catastrophe' was the finest of our victories. The one that made both of us face the inevitable solitude of the final encounter. That showed us our love and its time as a landscape which, once it has been experienced, becomes timeless and without end. 'The dead belong to no one', Diatkine told me in a session. This feeling of non-possession is crushing, but also superior in every way to the possessions and dispossessions of reality. 'Our secret is in music', you wrote to me in 1983. The moment of the final note, the moment to return music to silence, is not natural. Barenboim expresses it well when he distinguishes between the death of a natural sound – the end of the sound of rain or wind – and the end of a musical sound. The latter is physically carried, held and rested, like a body, by the musician. In writing to you today, I relive the physical effort of separation, of the return to silence. Artificially, slowly, my words return you to the absence of sound. Yes, our secret was in music. And music is linked to prayer. In the sense that you don't have to believe in God to pray. I would even say that the most beautiful of prayers dispenses with God. It simply asks that which is not the self to reduce the importance of the self. This is what I do in leaving you at the end of this page. I reduce us, you and me, in favour of an us that worked wonders. I say goodbye to the ideal. In place of which, I look at a fruit tree in blossom which particularly excites me because I can imagine its branches blackened by winter in a few months' time. Naked. And I think, simply, as long as meaning is moving, we mustn't stop it.

NOTES

CHAPTER I

1. Theodor W. Adorno and Shierry Weber Nicholsen, 'Punctuation Marks', *The Antioch Review* 48, no. 3 (Summer 1990): 300–5.
2. Edward Said, *Beginnings: Intention and Method* (London: Granta, 2012), 21.
3. Ibid., 66.

CHAPTER II

1. Ibid., 379.
2. Daniel Barenboim and Edward Said, *Parallels and Paradoxes: Explorations in Music and Society* (New York: Pantheon Books, 2002), 68.
3. In French: 'Les Russes, la tragédie leur va, mais nous, les Roumains, les Libanais, la tragédie ne nous vaaaa paaas!'
4. Said, *Beginnings*, 66.
5. Albert Camus, *The Fall*, trans. Robin Buss (London: Penguin, 2006), 36.

CHAPTER III

1. Said, *Beginnings*, 50.
2. Ibid., 142.

3. Edward Said, *Joseph Conrad and the Fiction of Autobiography* (Cambridge: Harvard University Press, 1966).

4. The phrase used by André Green in my conversations with him. André Green, *La Lettre et la Mort. Promenade d'un psychanalyste à travers la littérature: Proust, Shakespeare, Conrad, Borges . . . Entretiens avec Dominique Eddé* (Paris: Denoël, 2012), 135.

5. Letter to Graham cited by Said in *Joseph Conrad and the Fiction of Autobiography*, 34.

6. Said, *Beginnings*, 73.

7. Letter cited by Said in *Joseph Conrad and the Fiction of Autobiography*, 33.

8. Said, *Joseph Conrad and the Fiction of Autobiography*, 140.

9. Virginia Woolf, *A Room of One's Own* (London: Penguin, 2000), 6.

10. Edward Said, *Culture and Imperialism* (London: Vintage, 1994), 198.

CHAPTER IV

1. André Green, *Joseph Conrad: Le premier commandement* (Paris: In Press, 2008).

2. Henry James, *Henry James: Selected Letters*, ed. Leon Edel (Cambridge: Harvard University Press, 1987), 368.

3. Green, *La Lettre et la Mort*, 136. (Translated for this edition.)

4. Ibid.

5. Said, *Beginnings*, 40.

6. Ibid., 71.

7. Edward Said, *The World, the Text and the Critic* (New York: Vintage, 1991), 55.

8. Green, *La Lettre et la Mort*, 135. (Translated for this edition.)

9. Jocelyn Baines, *Conrad: A Critical Biography* (London: Penguin Books, 1971), 23.

10. Said, *Joseph Conrad and the Fiction of Autobiography*, 98.

11. Baines, *Conrad*, 296.

12. Said, *Joseph Conrad and the Fiction of Autobiography*, 99.

13. Said, *Out of Place: A Memoir* (New York: Vintage, 1999), 149.

14. The existence of this unfinished text that I have never seen was revealed to me by Timothy Brennan, who is currently working on an intellectual biography of Edward Said.
15. Edward Said, *On Late Style: Music and Literature Against the Grain* (New York: Vintage, 2006).
16. Said, *On Late Style*, 5.
17. Oscar Wilde, *The Soul of Man under Socialism* (London: Black House, 2012), 40.
18. Joseph Conrad, *Heart of Darkness* (Oxford: Oxford University Press, 2002), 178.

CHAPTER V

1. Edward Said, *Culture and Imperialism* (New York: Knopf, 1993), 168.
2. Ibid., 277.
3. Edward Said, *Orientalism* (New York: Pantheon Books, 1978), 153.
4. Ibid., 180.
5. Ibid., 179.
6. See Gérard D. Khoury, 'Structures de pouvoir et structures familiales dans un pays méditerranéen: le cas libanais', *Relations internationales* 87 (Autumn 1996): 261–75.

CHAPTER VI

1. Said, *Out of Place*, 3.
2. Tidiane N'Diaye, *Le Génocide voilé* (Paris: Gallimard, 2017), 63.
3. Ibid., 189.
4. Elias Canetti, *Crowds and Power* (London: Victor Gollancz, 2000).
5. Said, *Culture and Imperialism*, 294.
6. *Maqsoud* means 'intended' or 'destined' in Arabic.
7. *Schuld* can translate as both 'guilt' and 'debt', but in the plural it means 'debts'.
8. Friedrich Nietzsche, *On the Genealogy of Morals*, trans. Walter Kaufmann and R. J. Hollingdale (London: Vintage, 1989), 62–3.

CHAPTER VII

1. Green, *La Lettre et la Mort*, 101.
2. Baines, *Conrad*, 24.
3. Said, *Out of Place*, 243.
4. Ibid., 93.
5. Ibid., 173.
6. Said, *On Late Style*, 66.
7. An American training camp established during the First World War.
8. Said, *Out of Place*, 9.
9. Ibid., 12.
10. Conrad, *Heart of Darkness*, 189.
11. Green, *Joseph Conrad*, 28. (Translated for this edition.)
12. Said, *Out of Place*, 140-1.
13. Ibid., 75.
14. Said, *Beginnings*, 106.
15. Said, *Joseph Conrad and the Fiction of Autobiography*.
16. Joseph Conrad, letter (originally in French) of 16 October to Marguerite Poradowska, *The Selected Letters of Joseph Conrad*, ed. Laurence Davies (Cambridge: Cambridge University Press, 2015), 21.
17. Said, *Out of Place*, 76.
18. Ibid., 292.
19. One is inevitably reminded of Albert Camus' *The Outsider*.
20. Said, *Out of Place*, 13.
21. Gilles Deleuze, *Difference and Repetition*, trans. Paul Patton (London: Continuum, 1994), 286.
22. Green, *Joseph Conrad*, 14. (Translated for this edition.)
23. Paper delivered at the conference 'Hommage à Edward Said' at the University of Paris 7 Denis Diderot, September 2004; cf. Dominique Eddé, 'Conrad, le "compagnon secret" de Said', *Tumultes*, no. 24 (May 2005): 215-23.
24. Joseph Conrad, *The Secret Sharer* (CreateSpace Independent Publishing Platform, 2011), 6.

25. Edward's maternal grandfather was a Baptist pastor in Nazareth.
26. Green, *Joseph Conrad*, 87. (Translated for this edition.)

CHAPTER VIII

1. Columbia University Press (website), 'Joseph Conrad and the Fiction of Autobiography', https://cup.columbia.edu/book/joseph-conrad-and-the-fiction-of-autobiography/9780231140058.
2. Said, *Beginnings*, 100.
3. Ibid., 149.
4. Ibid., 150.

CHAPTER IX

1. Said, *Out of Place*, 258–9.
2. Ibid., 261.
3. Ibid., 263.
4. Ibid., 264.
5. Ibid., 224.
6. Ibid., 280.
7. Ibid., 253.
8. Ibid.
9. Ibid., 254.
10. Ibid., 255.
11. Ibid.
12. Green, *Joseph Conrad*, 32. (Translated for this edition.)
13. Quotation from Coleridge in Said, *Beginnings*, 362.
14. Ibid.
15. Ibid. On Vico.
16. Jean-Paul Sartre, *Existentialism Is a Humanism*, trans. Philippe Mairet (New York: World Publishing Company, 1956). Available at: https://www.marxists.org/reference/archive/sartre/works/exist/sartre.htm
17. Said, *Beginnings*, 358.
18. Said, *Beginnings*, 361.

19. Ibid., 360.

20. Joseph Conrad, letter of 4 May 1918 to Barret H. Clark, *The Selected Letters of Joseph Conrad*, ed. Laurence Davies (Cambridge: Cambridge University Press, 2015), 390.

21. Said, *Out of Place*, 295.

22. Said, *Joseph Conrad and the Fiction of Autobiography*, 88.

CHAPTER X

1. This was how Foucault described his work in an interview with Roger-Pol Droit in 1975.

2. Michel Foucault, *Dits et écrits*, II (Paris: Gallimard, 2001), 687. (Translated for this edition.)

3. Karim Émile Bitar and Robert Fadel, eds, *Regards sur la France Trente spécialistes internationaux dressent le bilan de Santé de l'Hexagone* (Paris: Le Seuil, 2007), 108. (Translated for this edition.)

4. Michel Foucault, *Histoire de la folie à l'âge classique* (Paris: Gallimard, 1972), 649. (Translated for this edition.)

5. Michel Foucault, *History of Madness*, trans. Jonathan Murphy and Jean Khalfa (London: Routledge, 2006), 46.

6. Jacques Derrida, *Writing and Difference*, trans. Alan Bass (London: Routledge and Kegan Paul, 1978), 61.

7. Ibid., 76.

8. Said, *The World, the Text and the Critic*, 215.

9. Ibid., 214.

10. Sonia Dayan-Herzbrun, 'De Frantz Fanon à Edward Said', *Journal of French and Francophone Philosophy* 19, no. 1 (2011): 73. (Translated for this edition.)

11. Ibid., 72.

12. Ibid., 71–81.

13. Bitar and Fadel (eds), *Regards sur la France*, 108. (Translated for this edition.)

14. Edward Said, *Reflections on Exile: And Other Literary and Cultural Essays* (London: Granta, 2000), 88.

15. Ibid.

16. Giambattista Vico, *La Science nouvelle* (Paris: Gallimard, 1993), 146.

17. Michel Foucault, *Language, Counter-memory, Practice: Selected Essays and Interviews* (Ithaca: Cornell University Press, 1977), 214.

18. Said, *Beginnings*, 179.

CHAPTER XI

1. Ibid., 81.

2. Ibid.

   Ibid., 82. Sunan an-Nasa'i, Book 19, Hadith 23: '*Kull bid'a ḍalāla wa kull ḍalālatin fī l–nār*', 'Every innovation is going astray and every going astray will be in the Fire.'

3. Jacqueline Chabbi, *Les Trois piliers de l'islam. Lecture anthropologique du Coran* (Paris: Le Seuil, 2016), 351. (Translated for this edition.)

4. Ibid., 176.

5. Said, *Réflexions sur l'exil*, 133. (Translated for this edition.)

6. Ibid., 89.

7. Interview with Hamid Barrada in *Le Nouvel Observateur*, 1990.

8. Edward Said, *Covering Islam: How the Media and the Experts Determine How We See the Rest of the World* (New York: Random House, 1981), xv.

9. Edward Said, *Representations of the Intellectual* (London: Vintage, 1994).

CHAPTER XII

1. Maxime Rodinson, *Europe and the Mystique of Islam*, trans. Roger Veinus (London: IB Tauris, 2002), 131.

2. Cited in Youssef Courbage and Manfred Kropp, eds, *Penser l'Orient. Traditions et actualités des orientalistes français et allemand* (Bayreuth: Orient-Institut, 2009).

3. The only exceptions to the rule were Éric Hazan and Évelyne Cazade with the publication of *Israël, Palestine: l'égalité ou rien* (Paris: La Fabrique, 1999) and *Des intellectuels et du Pouvoir* (Paris: Le Seuil, 1996).

4. Abdirahman A. Hussein, *Edward Said: Criticism and Society* (London: Verso, 2004).

CHAPTER XIII

1. Said, *Culture and Imperialism*, 172.
2. George Orwell, review of *Spanish Testament* by Arthur Koestler, *Time and Tide*, 5 February 1938.
3. See Said, *Reflections on Exile*.
4. Ibid., 94.
5. Said, *The World, the Text and the Critic*, 75.
6. 'Interview with Charles Glass', *Edward Said: The Last Interview*, directed by Michael Dibb (Brooklyn: Icarus Films, 2004). 'A lot of people I admired were deeply unpleasant. Conrad, who is the great figure of my imaginative life, was also a deeply unpleasant man.'
7. Said, *The World, the Text and the Critic*, 76.
8. Said, *Reflections on Exile*, 96.
9. Said, *The World, the Text and the Critic*, 77.
10. Simon Leys, *Orwell ou l'horreur de la politique* (Paris: Flammarion, 2014), 65. (Translated for this edition.)
11. Ibid., 30.
12. Ibid.
13. Said, *Reflections on Exile*, 95.
14. He told K E Bitar, 'For me Sartre is one of the world's greatest intellectuals of the 20th century.' Bitar and Robert Fadel (eds), *Regards sur la France*, 104. (Translated for this edition.)
15. Said, *The World, the Text and the Critic*, 83.
16. Said, *Orientalism*, 251–2.
17. George Orwell, *Some Thoughts on the Common Toad* (London: Penguin, 2010).
18. Leys, *Orwell ou l'horreur de la politique*. (Translated for this edition.)
19. Said, *Reflections on Exile*, 97.
20. George Orwell, *1984* (London: Penguin, 1954), 54.
21. Jean-Paul Sartre, *Being and Nothingness: An Essay on Phenomenological Ontology*, trans. Hazel Barnes (London: Routledge, 2003), 82 ff.

22. Albert Camus, *Algerian Chronicles*, trans. Arthur Goldhammer (Cambridge: Harvard University Press, 2013), 14.

23. Cited in Said, *Culture and Imperialism*, 179.

24. Conrad, *Heart of Darkness*, 107.

25. Alphonse de Lamartine, *De Lamartine's Visit to the Holy Land or, Recollections of the East,* trans. Thomas Phipson (London: George Virtue, 1847), 344.

26. Thomas Hughs, *The Universal Class-Book: Being a Selection of Pieces, in Prose and Verse, Designed for the Use of the Higher Classes in Schools* (Philadelphia: Uriah Hunt, 1830), 197.

27. François-René de Chateaubriand, *Œuvres complètes de Chateaubriand* (Paris: P H Krabbe, 1852), 231. (Translated for this edition.)

28. Bitar and Fadel (eds), *Regards sur la France*, 117. (Translated for this edition.)

29. Ibrahim A. Abu-Lughod, Roger Heacock and Khaled Nashef, *The Landscape of Palestine: Equivocal Poetry* (Birzeit: Birzeit University Publications, 1999), 153.

30. Albert Camus, *The Plague*, trans. Robin Buss (London: Penguin, 2002), 65, 43.

31. Albert Camus, 'The Adulterous Woman', in *Exile and the Kingdom*, trans. Justin O'Brien (London: Penguin, 2006).

32. Jean-Paul Sartre, *The Flies*, trans. Stuart Gilbert (London: Hamish Hamilton, 1946).'

33. Camus, *Algerian Chronicles*, 53. The article 'Famine in Algeria' was written immediately after the massacres at Sétif in May 1945. The French army's suppression of anticolonialist and nationalist demonstrations killed several thousand Muslim Algerians – between 8,000 and over 30,000, the numbers are still disputed.

34. Frantz Fanon, *The Wretched of the Earth*, trans. Constance Farrington (London: Penguin, 2001), 40.

35. Said, *Culture and Imperialism*, 323.

36. There was reason to worry at the funeral of Hrant Dink, the Armenian intellectual murdered in Istanbul in 2007. Among the tens of thousands of people in the streets, there was not one veiled woman.

CHAPTER XIV

1. I felt this humiliating indulgence like a vicious slap in 1989, when Bernard Pivot invited the Lebanese killer Joseph Saadé onto his talk show *Apostrophes*. This was a man who had avenged the death of his sons by massacring 400 anonymous Muslims, a slaughter combined with unspeakable torture and humiliation. He was not a Muslim, but he was Lebanese. That was enough for him not to be seen as part of the 'civilised' world. The programme was calmly called 'Par qui le scandale arrive' ('By Whom Offence Comes') and the 'offence' was illustrated in the credit sequence by Géricault's *Raft of the Medusa* and Manet's *Déjeuner sur l'herbe*. That's all. Could we have imagined for a single second that the memories of a German or French mass murderer would have been introduced by these masterpieces? Among the other guests, supposedly embodying 'offences' comparable to that of the Lebanese killer, were Monseigneur Jacques Gaillot, a bishop whose courageous positions had cost him dear, and Christian Laborde, regarded as a provocative novelist for young adults. At the time, I reacted by publishing a critical piece in *Le Monde*, saying more or less what I have just said here, and which earned me reprisals of a kind I leave to the imagination. This story is a perfect example of the French orientalism from which Edward Said also suffered.

2. Sophie Bessis, *La Double impasse: L'universel à l'épreuve des fondamentalismes religieux et marchand* (Paris: La Découverte, 2014), 179–80. (Translated for this edition.)

3. Michel Foucault, *Le Courage de la vérité: Le gouvernement de soi et des autres, II* (Paris: Le Seuil, 2009), 328. (Translated for this edition.)

4. Bitar and Fadel (eds), *Regards sur la France*, 80.

5. Ibid., 81.

6. Frantz Fanon, *Black Skin, White Masks*, trans. Charles Lam Markmann (London: Pluto, 1986), 179–81.

7. Samir el Sayegh, *L'Art islamique. Lecture de sa philosophie et de ses caractéristiques esthétiques* (Dubai: Dar al Marefah, 1988), 414. (Translated for this edition.)

8. Said, *Reflections on Exile*, 93.
9. Ibid., 94.
10. Ibid., 98.
11. Ibid., 53.
12. Tariq Ali, *Conversations with Edward Said* (London: Seagull Books, 2006), 120.

CHAPTER XV

1. Friedrich Nietzsche, *On Truth and Lies in a Nonmoral Sense* (CreateSpace Independent Publishing Platform, 2015), 41–2.
2. Saul Friedländer, *Nazi Germany and the Jews: The Years of Persecution, 1933–1939* (London: Weidenfield & Nicholson, 1997).
3. Edward Said, 'Breaking the Deadlock: A Third Way', *Al Hayat*, 30 June 1998, and 'Israël-Palestine: Pour une troisième vie', *Le Monde diplomatique*, August 1998.

CHAPTER XVI

1. Said, *Reflections on Exile*, 29.
2. 'I should have chosen any language but French, for I am out of tune with its air of distinction, it is at the opposite pole from my nature and my excesses, my true self and my kind of miseries. Through its rigidity and the elegant sum of constraints it represents, it appears to me as an exercise in asceticism or rather as a combination of straitjacket and salon.' E. M. Cioran, *Exercices d'admiration: Essais et portrait* (Paris: Gallimard, 1986). (Translated for this edition.)
3. Said, *Representations of the Intellectual*, 55.
4. E. M. Cioran, *Anathemas and Admirations*, trans. Richard Howard (New York: Arcade Publishing, 2012), 91.
5. Ibid.
6. Ibid., 95.

CHAPTER XVII

1. Marcel Proust, *Pleasures and Days*, trans. Andrew Brown (London: Alma Classics, 2013), 106.

CHAPTER XIX

1. Said, *Culture and Imperialism*, 323.
2. Said, *Beginnings*, 81. On modern Arabic literature before the twentieth century, 'The desire to create an alternative world, to modify or augment the real world through the act of writing (which is one motive underlying the novelistic tradition in the West) is inimical to the Islamic world view . . . Islam views the world as a plenum, capable of neither diminishment nor amplification.'
3. Joseph Conrad, *Nostromo* (Oxford: Oxford University Press, 2009), 324.
4. The term 'signals of recognition' is André Green's.
5. Said, *Beginnings*, 126.
6. Ibid., 133.
7. Falk was said to have won his wife at cards, but the rumour was false. *Falk* is available from Project Gutenberg: http://www.gutenberg.org/ ebooks/493.
8. Said, *On Late Style*, 44.
9. Ibid., 47.
10. Edward Said, 'In the Chair', *London Review of Books*, 17 July 1997.

CHAPTER XX

1. Cited in *On Late Style*, 42.
2. Ibid., 157.
3. Ibid., 45.
4. Ibid., 71.
5. Ibid., 49.
6. Barenboim and Said, *Parallels and Paradoxes*, 42–3.
7. Edward Said, *Freud and the Non-European* (London: Verso, 2003), 28.

8. Said, *On Late Style*, 3.

9. Wallace Stevens, 'Mozart, 1935', *Wallace Stevens: Selected Poems* (New York: Knopf, 2009), 77.

10. Said, *On Late Style*, 87.

CHAPTER XXI

1. Edward Said, *The Politics of Dispossession: The Struggle for Palestinian Self-Determination, 1969-1994* (London: Vintage, 1995), 172.

2. Edward Said, 'The One-State Solution', *New York Times Magazine*, October 1999. This article is available online at nytimes.com.

3. Éric Hazan and Eyal Sivan, *Un État commun : Entre le Jourdain et la mer* (Paris: La Fabrique, 2012).

4. Zeev Sternhell, *The Founding Myths of Israel*, trans. David Maisel (Princeton: Princeton University Press, 1999), 43.

5. Edward Said, *The Politics of Dispossession* (New York: Vintage Books, 1995), 178.

6. Said, *The Politics of Dispossession*, 180.

7. In September 1999 *Commentary Magazine* published a defamatory article by Justus Reid Weiner.

8. Said, *The Politics of Dispossession*, 195.

9. Dominique Eddé, *Le Crime de Jean Genet* (Paris: Le Seuil, 2007).

10. Said, *The Politics of Dispossession*, 192.

11. Ibid., 198.

12. Ibid., 199.

CHAPTER XXII

1. Edward Said, *Music at the Limits* (London: Bloomsbury, 2009), 259.

2. *New York Times*, February 2000.

3. Barenboim and Said, *Parallels and Paradoxes*, 114.

4. Said, *Joseph Conrad and the Fiction of Autobiography*, 41.

5. Bitar and Fadel (eds), *Regards sur la France*, 82.

6. Aimé Césaire, *Cahier d'un retour au pays natal* (Paris: Présence

africaine, 1956). (Translated for this edition.)

7. Barenboim and Said, *Parallels and Paradoxes*, 111.

8. Ibid., 112.

9. The Divan Orchestra, comprising Israeli and Arab musicians, founded by Barenboim and Said in Weimar in 1999.

10. Barenboim and Said, *Parallels and Paradoxes*, 115.

11. Ibid., 117.

12. Said, *Music at the Limits*, 261.

13. Ibid., 261.

14. Kate Connolly, 'Daniel Barenboim Opens Berlin Music Academy for Middle East Students', *Guardian*, 8 December 2016.

15. Edward Said, *Musical Elaborations* (New York: Columbia University Press, 1992), 89.

16. Barenboim and Said, *Parallels and Paradoxes*, 117.

17. Ibid., 118–19.

18. Ibid., 119–20.

19. Ibid., 122.

20. Cited in Said, *Joseph Conrad and the Fiction of Autobiography*, 49.

21. Said, *On Late Style*, 24.

22. Theodor Adorno, *Aesthetic Theory*, trans. C. Lenhardt (London: Routledge and Kegan Paul, 1984), 140.

23. Barenboim and Said, *Parallels and Paradoxes*, 137.

24. Ibid., 122.

25. Ibid., 123.

26. Ibid.

27. Ibid.

28. Marcel Proust, *Les Lettres retrouvées* (Paris: Plon, 1966), 157. Cited by André Green in *La Lettre et la Mort*, 121. (Translated for this edition.)

29. Proust cited by Said in *Musical Elaborations*, 75.

30. Barenboim and Said, *Parallels and Paradoxes*, 133.

31. Charles Baudelaire, *The Flowers of Evil and Paris Spleen: Selected Poems*, trans. Wallace Fowlie (Mineola: Dover, 2012), 18.

32. Said, *Reflexions on Exile*, 509–10.

33. Said, *Music at the Limits*, 300.

34. Barenboim and Said, *Parallels and Paradoxes*, 133.

35. Ibid., 132–3.

36. Cited by Said in *Musical Elaborations*, 64.

37. Rainer Maria Rilke, *The Duino Elegies*, trans. Leslie Norris and Alan Keele (Rochester: Camden House, 2008), 3.

38. Barenboim and Said, *Parallels and Paradoxes*, 62.

39. Ibid., 145.

40. Ibid., 147.

41. Said, *Joseph Conrad and the Fiction of Autobiography*, 148.

42. Thomas Mann, *Le Docteur Faustus* (Paris: Albin Michel, 1962), 330.

43. Conrad, *Heart of Darkness*, 183.

44. Ibid., 182.

45. Ibid., 154.

46. Ibid., 127.

47. Ibid., 129.

48. Ibid.

49. Ibid., 153.

50. Ibid., 183.

51. Ibid., 184.

52. Ibid., 182.

CHAPTER XXIII

1. Said, *On Late Style*, 160.

INDEX